THE PSYCHOLOGY
OF THE CRIMINAL ACT
AND PUNISHMENT

THE PSYCHOLOGY
OF THE
CRIMINAL ACT
AND PUNISHMENT

Gregory Zilboorg, M.D.

HARCOURT, BRACE AND COMPANY
NEW YORK

Library of Congress Catalog Card Number: 54-6393

PRINTED IN THE UNITED STATES OF AMERICA

TO MARGARET STONE ZILBOORG
this is inscribed with affection and gratitude

CONTENTS

FOREWORD

ON MAY 6, 1953, in the city of Los Angeles, the American Psychiatric Association announced that I had been voted to be the recipient of the Isaac Ray Award for that year. This made me the second recipient of this award; the first was Dr. Winfred Overholser, the Superintendent of St. Elizabeths Hospital, who occupies the uncontested position of leadership in the field of forensic psychiatry in America.

The responsibility for this generous act on the part of the American Psychiatric Association in relation to this writer must rest, of course, on the shoulders of the Association, which is completing its one hundred and tenth year of working for and making American psychiatry what it is today. However, I do not want to give the impression that I wrote this little book without being fully cognizant that the responsibility for everything I have said in these pages is mine, solely. But my pen would not rest easily unless I used this opportunity to acknowledge my debt to the professional organization under whose aegis and in whose scientific climate I grew up as a medical man and a psychiatrist.

The honor and debt were further enhanced when the Committee on the Isaac Ray Award made the simultaneous announcement that Yale University had accepted the recipient of the award to deliver the Isaac Ray Lectures within its walls under the joint auspices of the Schools of Law and

Medicine. This is what the Isaac Ray Award is for: it strives to bring about a closer co-operation between the psychiatrist and the lawyer, and it wishes to foster the spirit of co-operation between the two from the time when they are still students and have not yet undergone that distortion of perspective which the practice of law without psychiatry and the practice of psychiatry without the benefit of legal psychology make so inevitable and so harsh on many human beings.

In this respect Yale, more than any university today, symbolizes the striving to bring about a healthy and humane synthesis between law and psychiatry. Yale has a special functional teaching unit for this purpose, a unit headed by a lawyer, my good friend George Dession, and a psychiatrist, also my good friend Dr. Lawrence Z. Freedman. To them a special acknowledgment is due for having jointly presided over the Isaac Ray Lectures, the outcome of which is this modest book.

The whole occasion was and is to us psychiatrists a solemn one, and I hope it is as solemn in the eyes of lawyers. Consequently, an expression of gratitude goes to President Griswold for his intellectual hospitality, and to Deans Sturges and Lippard for having opened the doors of their respective Schools to the Isaac Ray Lectures. I wish here also to thank my colleague Professor Frederick C. Redlich for his help and moral support—substantial, yet inconspicuous, as befitting a good psychiatrist.

The Yale lectures served me as an outline for this book; it is a small book, and it is far from doing full justice to the immense problem of love and hate as they are combined, refracted, and confused in the conflict which still exists after so many centuries between law and psychiatry.

No claim is made here that any panacea has been found. Rather it is claimed that it is our duty to open our eyes to the immensity of the problems involved, to their chronicity, to our tendency to drift around the issues instead of standing up to be counted. Also, it is hoped that our wonted but unjustified optimism about our being just will find itself considerably and justifiably chipped. It is also hoped that the writer will have succeeded here in repeating with some efficacy what so many have claimed before: that in matters of law or psychology, it is not enough to be correct or accurate; it is also mandatory to fuse our legal and psychiatric functions with a morality that is practiced, not merely given recognition.

The tedious job of verifying the factual references, of typing and proofreading was done by Miss Valerie Reich, who saved the writer a great deal of time, of energy, and of concern as to the accuracy of many points.

To my wife, Margaret Stone Zilboorg, special acknowledgment is due. The editorial and indexing efforts are always hers; but most of all, it is to her that I owe the inspiration for these pages. Without that inspiration I would have been unable to discharge my duty to the Committee on the Isaac Ray Award, to the American Psychiatric Association, to Yale University, and to my publishers who so generously support the work of the Isaac Ray Award by publishing the series of which this is the second volume.

GREGORY ZILBOORG, M.D.

New York, March, 1954.

THE PSYCHOLOGY
OF THE CRIMINAL ACT
AND PUNISHMENT

1.

THE NATURE AND THE QUALITY
OF THE ACT

THE EFFORTS made in recent years both by jurists and by psychiatrists to bring about a co-operative understanding between law and psychiatry are commendable and inspiring. These words are not merely a formal preliminary to a more formal discussion of a formal subject. They are spoken in an effort to give adequate voice to the spirit that unites us, lawyers and medical men, rather than to make a polite bow and then proceed to emphasize how absolutely and hopelessly different psychiatrists are from lawyers, and lawyers are from psychiatrists, and what bliss would be attained by the human community if all lawyers became confirmed psychiatrists at the same time as all psychiatrists became confirmed lawyers; if all criminals could be adequately punished in solid prisons of harsh discipline, and at the same time adequately treated by a host of psychiatrists and gradually cured of their alleged diseases called criminality.

Such utopian preconceptions are human of course, but the unity of psychiatry and the law cannot depend upon a utopia which hopes to establish a psychiatric kingdom of heaven on a juridical or criminal earth. Still less might we be justified in hoping that unity would be achieved by establishment of the heaven of jurisprudence on the psychiatric soil of a criminal earth. Nor can the much desired and hoped-for unity be attained by any verbal compromises, like that so happily attained by the often-quoted German professor of the history of religion who, not wishing to offend any of his audience, started his course by stating: "Gentlemen, some people believe in God, and some do not. We, in this course, will take the middle ground."

I shall promise to avoid the middle ground as judiciously as I am able to and as aptly as my psychiatric skill will permit me. I want to avoid the middle ground because this subject is a very serious one, and from time immemorial it has been treated with the zest of reformers, the passions of revolutionary missionaries, and the devotion of true believers. I would not want to abandon this truly sacred tradition, for ever since man began to punish man, there have been those who were ready to die for the right to punish, and those who were ready to die with the criminal for the right to save the condemned.

We need refer only to the circuses in which the believers in Christ were devoured, or to the bonfires of the sixteenth century. The spirit of these struggles remains the spirit of the history of the relationship between law and psychiatry, under whatever name these two disciplines have appeared during various centuries and eras. To emphasize this tradition does not mean to deny that ours is a much more humanized age. If it were not so humanized, I would not be able to speak my mind so freely here. Yet the very fact that the struggle seems attenuated makes it incumbent upon us not to overlook the true spirit of the eternal struggle between the striving to punish and the yearning to understand and to forgive, both within the same community of men, and more often than not within one and

the same person. Reverberations of this inner conflict are
to be found in the pronouncements of almost every older
as well as contemporary writer or jurist or practitioner
who has happened to be concerned with the problems of
crime and punishment, of law and psychiatry, of the medical expert and the lawyer, the jury and the prosecutor, the
judge and the mandatory clauses of the law.

Some of the characteristic aspects of this conflict are reflected in almost all authoritative statements of the past
and/or the present. An example:

In a speech on "Learning and Science" delivered on June
25, 1895, Oliver Wendell Holmes remarked:

The law, so far as it depends on learning, is indeed, as it has
been called, the government of the living by the dead. To a very
considerable extent no doubt it is inevitable that the living
should be so governed. The past gives us our vocabulary and fixes
the limits of our imagination; we cannot get away from it. There
is, too, a peculiar logical pleasure in making manifest the continuity between what we are doing and what has been done before. But the present has a right to govern itself so far as it can;
and it ought always to be remembered that historic continuity
with the past is not a duty, it is only a necessity.

I hope that the time is coming when this thought will bear
fruit. An ideal system of law should draw its postulates and its
legislative justification from science. As it is now, we rely upon
tradition, or vague sentiment, or the fact that we never thought
of any other way of doing things, as our only warrant for rules
which we enforce with as much confidence as if they embodied
revealed wisdom. Who here can give reasons of any different kind
for believing that half the criminal law does not do more harm
than good? Our forms of contract, instead of being made once for
all, like a yacht, on the lines of least resistance, are accidental relics
of early notions, concerning which the learned dispute. How
much has reason to do in deciding how far, if at all, it is ex-

pedient for the State to meddle with the domestic relations? And so I might go on through the whole law.[1]

This unconventional and almost rebellious statement, sober and daring as it is, harmonizes not too well with Holmes's attitude toward the criminal who is condemned to death. As he points out in one of his letters to Laski, the criminal who is about to die at the hands of the executioner appears to Holmes merely as the soldier of an army at war. The sacrifice seems to Holmes justified and even a patriotic necessity—as if it were the duty of the condemned to die for the greater glory of the law. This attitude hardly betrays the faith in science which he proclaimed elsewhere. In his letter to Laski of December 17, 1925, some thirty years after his proclamation of faith in science, Holmes says:

As to your doctors and judges on uncontrollable impulse I think the short answer is that the law establishes certain minima of social conduct that a man must conform to at his peril. Of course as I said in my book it bears most hardly on those least prepared for it, but that is what it is for. I am entirely impatient of any but broad distinctions. Otherwise we are lost in the maze of determinism. If I were having a philosophical talk with a man I was going to have hanged (or electrocuted) I should say, I don't doubt that your act was inevitable for you but to make it more avoidable by others we propose to sacrifice you to the common good. You may regard yourself as a soldier dying for your country if you like. But the law must keep its promises.[2]

Here the cleavage between the scientific and nonscientific attitudes toward the law appears not only as a flagrant con-

---

[1] From "Learning and Science," speech, June 25, 1895, in Oliver Wendell Holmes, *Collected Legal Papers*, Harcourt, Brace & Howe, 1920, pp. 138-39.

[2] Mark de Wolfe Howe, ed., *Holmes-Laski Letters*, Harvard University Press, 1953, p. 806.

tradiction but as a true confusion. This confusion does not appear self-evident at first, because the two mutually contradictory attitudes are separated by a considerable span of time, or chain of events. But contradiction there is, and it is an eternal contradiction the solution of which lies apparently in the inner psychology of the problem, and not in its formal logical sequences or semantic hairsplitting. It is my hope that in the course of the considerations which follow some light may be shed on this fundamental contradiction or, as we in our psychological age are wont to say, this fundamental conflict.

Another not uninteresting sampling: In a review of an article, Isaac Ray wrote in 1868: [3]

Whether [the person in question] subsequently served on a jury, as the writer states, we have not taken the trouble to ascertain. If he did, we dare to say he performed the duty acceptably, but we have not been so profoundly impressed with the wisdom of juries as to regard the fact as conclusive proof that he was not then, and never had been, insane. We doubt not that many of the inmates of our hospitals would perform the functions of a juryman as creditably as the average of men now put into the jury box. They do a great many other things requiring more forethought and steadiness than it does to say yes or no to a verdict as likely to be wrong as right.

Please note the tone of irony, even bitterness, in Isaac Ray's attitude toward juries. Isaac Ray, too, strove to introduce science, particularly medical science, into the courtroom, seeking thus to avoid emotional decisions which so often appear disguised as judicious decisions.

Isaac Ray was one of those unique personalities who was able to combine a cultivated mind and a high administra-

[3] *Atlantic Monthly*, August, 1868, p. 237.

tive ability, an excellent psychiatric endowment and a profound social consciousness. He wrote his book *A Treatise on the Medical Jurisprudence of Insanity* [4] (1838) six years before he was called to become the first superintendent of Butler Hospital (for mental diseases) in Providence, Rhode Island. Both his book and his administration of the hospital remain classic examples of steadfast service and devotion to an ideal. Isaac Ray spoke the language of the future as early as 1838. We today are still using Isaac Ray as a guide in many of our modern strivings.

Another example, this time from the pen of two contemporary medico-legal authorities: Manfred Guttmacher and Henry Weihofen. In their *Psychiatry and the Law* [5] they almost brazenly state that the relationship between the prosecutor and the medical expert is not a co-operative relationship in search for the truth, but a sort of joust, a boxing bout with few if any holds or fouls barred. It is a performance before a jury, and a harsh struggle of two men each of whom wants to win no matter what. This, written in 1952, is peculiarly reminiscent of the picture drawn in his day by Isaac Ray, except that in 1838 Ray was less disillusioned, more hopeful, more fervent in his faith and hope that both psychiatry and the law would some day treat one another with dignity, with mutual respect and humanitarian efforts for better, more just justice. This is what was paramount in Isaac Ray's mind, and this is what made him an almost prophetic pioneer.

In its issue of January, 1839, the *American Jurist* [6] published the following notice: "A charge to the Grand Jury

[4] Charles C. Little and James Brown, 1838.
[5] W. W. Norton, 1952.
[6] P. 458.

of Merrimack County, N.H. delivered at the September Term of the Court of Common Pleas, 1838 by the Hon. Joel Parker, Chief Justice of the State of New Hampshire; published in the *New Hampshire Patriot and State Gazette* of October 15, 22, and 29, 1838."

The notice mentions that Judge Parker

avails himself of the recently published work of Dr. Ray, on the medical jurisprudence of insanity, the general doctrines of which he adopts and sanctions. Our opinion of Dr. Ray's work, which we reviewed in our last July number, is already well known to our readers; and it affords us the highest gratification, to find that opinion strengthened and confirmed by the high authority of Chief Justice Parker. An expression of the private individual opinion of a man of learning and science, in favor of the new doctrine of insanity, we should regard as a most happy circumstance; but, in this charge of the highest judicial officer of New Hampshire, there are other and stronger grounds, upon which the friends of humanity and science have reason to congratulate themselves. We regard it as an official declaration, that the theory of insanity, which it recognises, is hereafter to be applied in the regulation of the insane, and in considering and judging of their rights and responsibilities, in the state of New Hampshire. In this point of view, it is fully equivalent to a legislative act. We earnestly hope, that other judges, laying aside all prejudice, and all preconceived theories, will be excited by the example of the chief justice of New Hampshire, to bestow upon this most important matter that consideration which it deserves.

It is well known that New Hampshire was a truly pioneering state in the matter of a psychiatric and not a purely legalistic approach to what is still mistakenly called insanity. Isaac Ray was quite close to Chief Justice Joel Parker, as he later was to Justice of the Supreme Court of New Hampshire the Hon. Charles Doe, who was to become Chief Justice of the Supreme Court of his state. However, the Charles

Doe period covered roughly the years 1859-1896, whereas
the years of Judge Parker's intellectual co-operation with
Isaac Ray are historically much more important. Those
were years during which American judges and their criminological orientation appeared to be more independent and
original than they became after 1845, that is to say, only
two years after the so-called McNaghten rule was formulated and later imported from England to lay claim on a
place in many statute books of many states in the Union.

The future historian will some day assess the true harm
which the McNaghten rule has done to justice as well as to
scientific criminology and forensic psychiatry, not only in
America but in England as well, and wherever English
criminal law is followed. At this juncture it will suffice to
say that, whether it happens to be on the statute books or
not, the McNaghten rule is substantially the guiding principle of our criminal jurisprudence whenever psychiatric
issues are raised. As such it stands almost immutable; it is
the impenetrable wall behind which sits entrenched the
almost unconquerable prosecutor; it is the monster of the
earnest psychiatrist which prevents him from introducing
into the courtroom true understanding of human psychology and of the psychology of the criminal act.

It may be argued, of course, that the court is not interested in psychological information or in any other scientific
data; the court's business, some insist, is not the administration of justice, but the administration of the law. I have
heard this statement repeatedly from many representatives
of the legal profession, on and off the bench, at and away
from the bar. This attitude is logical, reasonable, practical;
in my opinion it is also untenable, because it contains the
seeds of profound immorality. Of course, the law must be

administered, but in matters of crime and punishment must not the substantive aspects of human relations take precedence over the adjective ones, and must not the law always be coupled to the moral values of man?

Some may claim that it is not the business of the law to spread or expand justice. It may not be its business on every occasion to assess how just it is, but it appears to me undeniable that it is the business of the law always and ever to be on the lookout that it is not *un*just. The problem then is not how formally just a given decision of the court is in matters of crime and punishment, but that it avoided being substantially unjust. In order to be able to achieve this negative but priceless moral height, it is incumbent upon the court to understand fully the very substance of the act on which it is called upon to pass. In order to achieve this understanding, more and more psychological knowledge must be allowed to be admitted into the courtroom. There cannot be any limit for the inclusion, there ought not to be any formalistic grounds for the exclusion of any detail or aspect which would serve the deeper psychological understanding of the act representing a given crime on which the court sits in judgment.

A purely formal attitude in such matters appears incongruous, even when it makes itself evident in a simple newspaper item. Thus in August, 1953, an English newspaper, under the heading "Court Held in Mental Hospital," reported on a Lithuanian, Jonas Gedeika (40), a certified mental patient, who was charged at Long Grove Mental Hospital, Epsom, with murdering another patient, Edmund Bruk (40) an ex-member of the Polish land forces. Albert William Farrant, a staff nurse, said Bruk ran out of the kitchen with Gedeika after him.

"I tried to grab Gedeika," said Farrant, "but he was too quick for me. He hit Bruk with a chair. . . . I tried to get him off but he was too powerful. Other staff came and eventually we got him away."

Inspector R. McMullen said Gedeika told him it was an accident. Gedeika was sent to Old Bailey for trial.

Here we have a mentally ill person, whose illness is severe enough so that he is a committed patient in a government institution, and yet out of the institution he goes to be tried for murder and his mental condition tested in accordance with the McNaghten rule.

I don't know what the outcome of this case of the Crown *versus* Gedeika finally was; for purposes of what I have to say here, it does not matter.

Let me cite another example, which I owe to Mrs. R. Emmet of the United Kingdom Delegation to the United Nations, who is also a judge of a children's court in Southern England. She kindly permitted me to cite the experience which she related to me and which I gratefully record here.

A boy of eleven was brought to court on a charge of having knocked down and hurt an old lady with his bicycle. Things looked bad for the boy. He admitted the fact of his transgression and there appeared to be no extenuating circumstances. As a matter of fact, there was a circumstance that pointed to an even worse situation: it looked as if there had been ill will in the act, for the boy was riding his bicycle on the wrong side of the street when he hurt the old lady. It almost looked as if he had crossed the road for the purpose of hitting her. And with a simple "Yes, ma'am," the boy readily admitted that he had crossed the road to ride on the wrong side. The judge felt that she had no way of letting the boy go unpunished, when a thought suddenly occurred to her and she asked whether it had been raining shortly before it all happened. "Yes, ma'am." Were there puddles on the wrong side of the road? Yes, he had crossed to ride on the wrong side of the road because it was such fun to ride in the smooth, mirror-like puddles and mess up the clear and clean reflections of the sky and the clouds.

"What did you do?" I asked Mrs. Emmet. She answered, "I let him go. You see," she added, "you can do such things, you can take such things into consideration, in children's court. But as far as adults are concerned, it is not a matter of justice; it is a matter of administering the law." One cannot help but recall Justice Holmes's tart remark: "The law must keep its promises."

Judge Emmet was revealingly frank when she admitted recalling something about her own children before she asked the little defendant whether it had been raining just before the mishap occurred. In other words, the mother in the judge was able to place herself in the psychological position of her own child, and through this identification she was able to identify herself with the little defendant in front of her. The result was justice arrived at through a striking and rather sudden attainment of psychological understanding.

Needless to say it is not given to all of us simple mortals, and still less to all officers of the law, to have this gift of automatic yet understanding identification with a criminal or an "insane," or both. As a matter of fact, the professional psychology of the administrator of the law is such that he must avoid even a semblance of such an identification, for such identification might weaken his purely legal judgment. He must protect himself against any tendency he might discover within himself to put himself psychologically in the defendant's place. He must avoid any identification with the criminal, for he must establish the greatest possible psychological distance between himself and the criminal. It is to the jury that is left a certain latitude in this respect, and therefore the jury might even recommend clemency. But even the jury is frequently urged not to consider the consequences of the verdict; that is to say, the jury is often admonished to keep that psychological distance which is mistakenly called objectivity. It is not really objectivity; it is more an effort to keep estranged from the criminal, to avoid knowing him, to look only on what he has done, on the act he has committed, to avoid any shortening of the psychological distance between the criminal and those concerned with judging and adjudging him.

The reader can easily see that this psychological position of the law is very different from that of the psychiatrist, whose job it is to delve into the deeper motives, the inner substance of the act for which the defendant is standing trial. Here we have one of the roots of the perennial conflict between psychiatry and the law. The law seems to be afraid that psychiatry might understand the transgressor too well, and might forgive too readily. Psychiatry seems to be afraid that the law actively avoids any true psychological understanding of the transgressor, because the law's business is to keep its punitive promises and not wax sentimental by way of scientific understanding.

Please note that I am merely pointing out here the essential fact of the conflict between law and psychiatry. For the time being I do not even attempt to pass judgment on the social or moral validity of this conflict. It suffices for the present to become fully aware of this active, dynamic conflict, which operates incessantly among the various agencies and personalities involved in the discovery, apprehending, trying, and finally pronouncing a verdict over and sentencing of a criminal. In other words, the smoothest machinery of justice suffers from the clogging influences of this psychological conflict.

During the tragic age of justice by fire there were many in the medical profession (even at that early period) who sensed intuitively this psychological conflict between law and human understanding, and many judges, too. There have been lawyers and physicians who through generations and centuries struggled for some solution of this conflict, for some resolution of the confusion that exists in the administration of justice. For many centuries this struggle was based primarily on the intuitive perception of the conflict. Its meaning and its psychological structure could not be grasped until very recent decades, during which the understanding of man's personality reached heretofore unsuspected depths. However, it is certainly too early to assume that this new understanding has brought us to a satisfactory, concrete solution of the conflict. It is a matter of regret, of course, but it is also a matter of historical and sociological fact that this solution is still rather distant, far out of our reach.

Something seems to be in the way. There seems to be some inner obstacle which beclouds the issue in the eyes of the well-meaning lawyer, the humanitarian judge, the judicious physician. It is difficult if not impossible to describe this obstacle in plain words, in plastic detail. All that is possible at this juncture is to illustrate the confusion, and thus inferentially to demonstrate the existence and the enormity of this obstacle.

Let us recall for a moment one of the most salient features of the McNaghten rule, which seems to be the best and thus far the most stable expression of our medico-juridical confusion. The capacity to distinguish, or rather to know, right from wrong is a feature of the rule both in England and in the United States. This is mistakenly and wrongfully known as the "right and wrong test," which test existed over a hundred years before the McNaghten rule was offered us. It is not a test, actually; it is a demand based upon an artificial definition of a nonexistent condition called "legal insanity." While the wording of the rule varies frequently, its constant or most frequent feature is this: "To establish a defence on the ground of insanity, it must be clearly proved that at the time of committing the act the party accused was labouring under such a defect of reason from disease of the mind as not to know the nature and quality of the act he was doing, or, if he did know it, that he did not know he was doing what was wrong." [7]

What is meant by "the nature and quality of the act"? These words are used with great solemnity in every criminal trial in which insanity is interposed as a defense. I have never heard or read any definition of the meaning of these words; as a matter of fact, they seem to be taken as so self-understood that they are used both to formulate the definition of and the test for legal insanity. What is the specific tangible meaning of *the nature* of the act? Certainly not the metaphysical, transcendental meaning of the act. The average man, even if he be a willful murderer, is not expected to be a well-versed metaphysician. We must assume that by "nature of the act" we mean the cruelty, the enormity, the

[7] This is the Maudsley version of the rule taken from his *Responsibility in Mental Disease,* D. Appleton, 1874.

immorality of it. If our assumption as to this moral connotation of the words "the nature of the act" is wrong, then
these words have no meaning whatsoever, not any longer
at any rate, if ever they had one.

Let us turn to the term *quality*. What are we to assume
is the self-understood meaning of the words "the quality
of the act"? Do they mean to connote something like a
modality in the philosophical, Leibnizian sense? The average man, even if he be a willful murderer, is not expected
to be a well-versed epistemologist. We must assume that by
"the quality of the act" is meant the inhuman, antihuman
immorality of the act. If our assumption as to the moral
connotation of these words is wrong, then these words have
no meaning whatsoever, not any longer at any rate, if ever
they had one.

It is obvious that the semantic obscurity of this aspect of
the McNaghten rule is due to the fact that the "rule" in-
tends to apply purely moralistic criteria to a clinical or scientific problem of a certain type or degree of mental disease. These moralistic criteria are the expression of man's
horror of the revolting act of murder, but they are disguised
in the formalistic, quasi-metaphysical dress of centuries
gone by, which one is asked to accept as a judicial formula
of logic and law. Under the circumstances, the presence of
confusion is not surprising; its absence would be. For even
here in the McNaghten formula, phrased by eminent judges,
we see sufficiently clearly reflected the struggle between
morality (which always threatens to carry with it some compassion) and an objectivity which becomes purely verbal
and therefore rather hollow. No wonder not only physicians
have risen often to criticize the McNaghten rule. Great
jurists have also occasionally risen against it. Sir James

Stephen was one of them. Almost three-quarters of a century ago, he stated his dissatisfaction with the rule and added: "I cannot help feeling . . . and I know some of the most distinguished judges of the Bench have been of the same opinion, that the authority of the answers is questionable." [8] According to Stephen these answers [9] (the McNaghten rule is one of them) "leave untouched every state of fact."

Contemporary lawyers and physicians have no difficulty in following Sir James Stephen, yet no solution of the problem has yet been found. We all, or almost all, agree that the method under discussion is deficient, but no sufficiently workable change has as yet been suggested. Here is an example of our earnest but inefficient groping in the matter. The President of the Royal College of Physicians, Dr. W. Russell Brain, was moved to write a letter to the London *Times,* and it reads in part as follows:

The . . . confusion arose from the unfortunate introduction of the term "insanity" into the trial. This is a word which has no clear medical, nor, I believe, legal meaning. It appears to have been used in the broad sense in which it is applied to a severe mental affection acquired after adolescence, in distinction from mental defect, by which is understood a mental affection present from birth or acquired during childhood. In this sense it was stated that Straffen [the criminal under discussion] was not "insane." This, however, was irrelevant: the true question was whether he was "of unsound mind," and the correct answer was that he was, since a mental defective is as much a person of unsound mind as someone suffering from a mental affection which has developed during adult life. Even if Straffen had been found to be a person of unsound mind, it might have made no differ-

---

[8] *History of Criminal Law in England,* London, 1883.

[9] The McNaghten rule was first given as one of the thirteen answers propounded to the judges of England by the House of Lords, *after* the case of McNaghten had been adjudicated.

ence to the verdict. The McNaghten rules require that if a person is to escape responsibility for his criminal act it must be proved, not only that he was of unsound mind at the time, but also that, either he did not know the nature and quality of his act, or that, if he did, he did not know that it was wrong. Straffen was found guilty because the medical evidence was quite definite that he knew both what he was doing and that he was wrong.

Many psychiatrists during recent years have criticized the McNaghten rules on the ground that, being over a century old, they take no account of modern knowledge of the mind. Between full responsibility there are many gradations; and responsibility should nowadays be related solely to intellectual knowledge. What of those who know what they are doing, and that it is wrong, but through medical disease fail to control their actions? Difficulties arise, however, when theory has to be translated into practice, for, whereas it is usually easy for a doctor to decide whether a man knew what he was doing and that it was wrong, it might be beyond the power of both doctor and jury to know whether he could have exercised enough self-control to have prevented himself from doing it.

The time has surely come to determine afresh in what circumstances mental illness should mitigate criminal responsibility. This is a question, not for lawyers or doctors, but for society to decide: it should then be possible for the experts to devise tests which are not only consonant with justice, but sufficiently clear and simple for use in its daily administration. A Royal Commission might well be the best way of attaining these ends.[10]

Dr. Brain's suggestion would turn over the solution of some medico-psychological and ethico-legal questions not to medicine, nor to the law, but to society as a whole, which is the most metaphysical entity known. And then he would ask medicine and the law to become the carpenters of a

[10] Letter to the Editor of the *Times* by W. Russell Brain, Royal College of Physicians, of August 30, 1952, published in the *Times* of Monday, Sept. 1, 1952: "The Straffen Case. Need for Inquiry into the Law."

medico-legal structure, the plans and specifications for which had been drawn by an anonymous society whose knowledge and experience in medico-legal architecture has always been known to be deficient.

True, Dr. Brain does optimistically suggest an inquiry by a special Royal Commission. Well, a report of the Royal Commission on Capital Punishment was published in the latter part of September, 1953. This report, which it took four years to prepare, states that "there is no sharp dividing line between sanity and insanity"; it would amend the McNaghten rule by adding "disorder of emotion" to the "defect of reason" as consequence of a disease of the mind. Such a conception of the disease of the mind would suggest that "insanity" might make it impossible for a man to refrain from a criminal act even if his reason told him the act was wrong.

This is undoubtedly a step forward, or rather a gesture in the direction of modern psychological knowledge of man, but it leaves the body of the McNaghten rule almost intact, and it would add a new responsibility for the jury to discharge. The Royal Commission would seem to recommend that the jury be burdened with the question of whether a given act was premeditated or not; it would have the jury not only bring out a verdict but take more definite part in sentencing the criminal. Here again, as in Dr. Brain's letter, we observe the tendency to turn over to the jury (society) those most intricate and confusing problems which both the law and psychiatry seem unable to solve—a step, if adopted, of doubtful advance. For after all, society is a disindividual-ized thing. It is public opinion, hence something quite unstable. Its ebbs and flows are unpredictable at times, and at times deleterious to truth and even to society itself. Such matters as law and justice, while rooted in the intuitive depths of public morality, cannot be permitted to depend upon the changing tide of public opinion, which is apt to be fickle. Such matters as scientific fact, particularly psychological scientific data, cannot be settled by a majority vote. Moreover, public opinion seldom if ever espouses a truth of science without many preliminary battles for the preservation of its own prejudices and even superstitions. And scientific truth itself, when caught in the cobwebs of public opinion, becomes stifled, its own face distorted and its own goals obscured.

One of the most poignant examples of this process is to be found in the Soviet penal code and its relation to psychiatry. On the one hand Soviet justice is strictly Marxist. It rejects the principle of free will. It is materialistic and deterministic, and yet it recognizes the personal responsibility of the criminal for his acts. It recognizes various degrees of guilt and punishment, and it has developed an intricate system which seems entangled with a sort of combination of predestination and free will, of rational, materialistic ethics and inarticulate moral imperatives. One even finds actual reverberations of the McNaghten rule in the Soviet code.[11] And when Soviet psychiatric thought comes up against a problem in which political motivations and incensed public opinion demand a punitive stand, it yields abjectly no matter how well; its scientific retreat is covered with the armamentarium of technical terminology. This is thrown in particular relief when one reads the Soviet psy-

[11] Frederick W. Killian and Richard Arens, "Use of Psychiatry in Soviet Criminal Proceedings, Parts I and II," *Journal of Criminal Law and Criminology of Northwestern University*, Vol. 41, No. 2, July-August, 1950, and Vol. 41, No. 4, November-December, 1950.

chiatric conclusions in the case of Rudolf Hess at the Nuremberg trial.

It will be recalled that at the outset of the Nuremberg proceedings, Hess had claimed emotional and mental illness, rendering him incapable of preparing his defense. His counsel had made application for his examination by Swiss psychiatrists. In denying the application, the tribunal had appointed a commission of British, American, French and Soviet psychiatrists and neurologists to report on his mental state. A British, a joint American and French, and a Soviet report were respectively submitted to the tribunal in due course. Agreement was reached by all three on the major issue posed by the inquiry. In almost identical language the reports rejected the contention of insanity while conceding the presence of a degree of amnesia which might prove handicapping to the defense. In submitting the most elaborate report of all, the Soviet medical delegation had made these points:

1. Delusions of persecution experienced by the defendant are not symptomatic of schizophrenic paranoia. [sic] They are explainable instead in terms of a "psychogenic paranoic reaction, that is, the psychologically comprehensible reaction of an unstable (psychologically) personality to the situation . . ."

2. The defendant's amnesia, though genuine, is not the result of mental disease, but is of hysterical origin of "a conscious-intentional (simulated) character," [sic] which in view of his sanity at the time of his flight to England "does not exonerate him from his responsibility under the indictment."

By way of formal conclusions, the Soviet medical delegation pronounced Hess "not insane in the strict sense of the word," adjudged him "an unstable person, which in technical terms is called a psychopathic personality," declared his amnesia to be genuine albeit a product of hysterical tendencies, and recommended narco-analysis for a clarification of the situation.[12]

12 Nazi Conspiracy and Aggression, Office of United States Chief of Counsel for Prosecution of Axis Criminality, Vol. 1, pp. 97-105 (194). Quoted by Frederick W. Killian and Richard Arens, *op. cit.,* p. 427.

This yielding of the truth to the pressure of public sentiment, this acceptance of a perverted scientific position by a
tribunal of justice, is not limited to Communist legal practice. I recall in this connection a case of a frightful crime,
one of the most gruesome murders ever committed in America. The defendant, a man of about sixty, was obviously
a mentally ill person whose illusion was of many years'
standing. Public opinion had been aroused by the crime
and the abhorrently pathological personality of the criminal. The psychiatric experts presented their views in as
honest a way as they knew. It transpired that for years the
defendant had been wont to add some human excreta to
his food. The expert who testified for the prosecutor was a
well-known psychiatrist of established professional and academic reputation. On cross-examination, the expert considered the addition of excreta to one's own food as not
abnormal at all and not indicative of any mental illness;
in confirmation he cited (without giving names, of course)
the case of one of his own patients (*sic*), a prominent businessman, who did the same thing with his salad often, or
even daily.

Let there be no misunderstanding; the flagrant error of
judgment on the part of this psychiatrist is not to be charged
to dishonesty, venality, and charlatanism—all qualities with
which, at least privately, some of the legal profession are
wont to charge most of the psychiatric profession. I have
no defense for this psychiatrist. I disapprove of his testimony most vigorously. But in justice to him it must be
said that he was a conscientious witness; he thought he
was being faithful to his oath, but he was also a victim of
the pressure of public opinion which judges the act and
not the person, and he spoke a monstrous incongruity on

the witness stand, helping to send a man to his death for a horrible crime. We need not assume that the court, the jury, and the attorneys were so naïve as to believe the truth of his testimony, but the court and the prosecutor and the jury accepted it as expert scientific appraisal of fact. The Court of Appeals read it in the printed report of the trial and did not single it out as something uniquely untrue or wrong. All this, because people were too aroused to dare to view an awful crime without separating it from the living derelict; they wanted to get rid of the doer as quickly as possible in order to forget the awful deed.

What is to be expected from modern psychiatry is an understanding not merely of the deeds but also of the doers. Only a proper understanding of the doers may enable us to find ways and means to prevent or to forestall the dreadful deeds. To seek this understanding is not only a privilege vouchsafed by the Lord to men of science, but also, I believe, the obligation of the law. My belief is not new; even as early as about a century ago the English psychiatrist Maudsley called attention to the necessity for an understanding of the true, inner psychological motivations which lead a man to commit murder. Freud was still a very young man when Maudsley attempted to demonstrate the need for psychological insight in the exercise of the criminal law. The role of the unconscious in human behavior had not yet been discovered, but Maudsley had a keen insight into the problem and he cited the following instructive example:

"I may quote the case of Burton, who was tried at the Maidstone Lent Assizes, in 1863, for murder. It was very simple and very shocking. The prisoner was a youth of eighteen years of age; his mother had been twice in a lunatic asylum, having been desponding, and having attempted suicide; his brother was of weak intellect, silly and peculiar. He himself was of low mental organization, and the person to whom he was apprenticed and others gave evidence that he was always strange, and not like other boys; he 'had a very vacant look, and when told to do anything, would often run about looking up to the sky as if he were a maniac;' so that the indentures were cancelled. The prisoner said that he had felt 'an impulse to kill someone;' that he sharpened his knife for the purpose, and went out to find someone whom he might kill; that he followed a boy, who was the first person he saw, to a convenient place; that he knocked him down, stuck him in the neck and throat, knelt upon his belly, grasped him by the neck, and squeezed till the blood came from his nose and mouth, and then trampled upon his face and neck until he was dead. He then washed his hands, and went quietly to a job which he had obtained. He knew the boy whom he had murdered, and had no ill-feeling against him, 'only I had made up my mind to murder somebody': he did it because he wished to be hanged. His counsel argued that this vehement desire to be hanged was the strongest proof of insanity; the counsel for the prosecution, on the other hand, urged that the fact of his having done murder in order to be hanged, showed clearly that he knew quite well the consequences of his act, and was therefore criminally responsible. He was found guilty; and Mr. Justice Wightman, in passing sentence, informed him that he had been 'found guilty of a more barbarous and inhuman murder than any which had come under my cognisance during a judicial experience of upwards of twenty years. It is stated,' the judge went on to say, 'that you laboured under a morbid desire to die by the hands of justice, and that for this purpose you committed the murder. This morbid desire to part with your own life can hardly be called a delusion; and, indeed, the consciousness on your part that you could effect your purpose by designedly depriving another of life, shows that you were perfectly able to understand the nature and consequences of the act which you were committing, and that you knew it was a crime for which by law the penalty was capital. This was, in truth, a further, and I may say a deeper, aggravation of the crime!' When sentence of death had been passed, the prisoner, who during the trial had been the least concerned person in court, said, with a smile, 'Thank you, my lord,' and went down from the dock, 'followed by an audible murmur, and almost a cry of horror from a densely crowded audience.' He was in due course executed; the terrible example having been thought necessary in order to deter others from doing murder out of a morbid desire to indulge in the gratification of being hanged." [13]

Maudsley then remarks: "If the example of Burton's execution was to have a deterrent effect, this effect ought to have been specially exerted upon those who were in a similar state of mind and troubled with similar morbid desires; and yet it is plain that on such persons it would have had a directly opposite effect, it would have stimulated them to do murder, by strengthening the insane motive which instigated it—the desire to be hanged."[14]

In other words, "the nature and the quality of the act" has no meaning whatsoever unless we bring it into harmony with the total personality of the criminal, even and particularly if it is the insane harmony of a pathological mind.

[13] Henry Maudsley, *op. cit.*, pp. 157-59.
[14] *Ibid.*, pp. 160, 161.

2.

THE DETERRENT EFFECT OF
PUNISHMENT

I N MAUDSLEY's example which I have just cited, the doubtful fate of the hope for a deterrent effect of execution should cause us no surprise. There is much yet to be said about the psychology of this goal, which has been for centuries called "the deterrent effect." No realistic results can be brought forward to support the claims of the principle of "the deterrent effect." We have only our inalienable faith that man can frighten man into decency, goodness, or at least moral neutrality. Even the realistic Justice Holmes was unable to master this faith. Perhaps it can be justified, but only in the small sphere of simple human relations, too simple to be of any social consequence. We shall return later to the psychology of this problem, when we can discuss it more dispassionately and more fruitfully. In the meantime, one more example:

"Lord Nugent mentions that in May 1840, a man named Thomas Templeman was executed at Glasgow for the murder of his wife, and that pickpockets plied their trade under the gallows; at that time, to be sure, a boy could not be hanged for stealing a pocket-handkerchief—a humane amendment had substituted transportation for life, and scores have been so transported; but Barrington, the *facile princeps* of the profession, declares that even when the offence was capital, the thieves selected the moment when the strangled man was swinging above them, as their happi-

[27]

est opportunity, because, they shrewdly agreed, 'Everybody's eyes were on one person, and all were looking up.' " [1]

Barrington may have been the greatest pickpocket in the history of man, but he knew nothing about the psychology of pickpockets. His explanation is too facile, too obvious, and too untrue. As we go along we shall endeavor to learn a little more about why the pickpockets were not deterred from committing their crimes even by the very sight of a criminal strangled and swinging from the gallows. Suffice it for the moment to say this: there is no scientific way of verifying the deterrent effect on the criminal of a given punishment, even of capital punishment. Moreover, statistical data such as those available for Sweden, for instance, covering the period from 1754-1942 seem to refute the claim that capital punishment has any deterrent effect at all on the murderer to be. A recent sociological study,[2] on the basis of careful examination of available data, states bluntly that "the results of the foregoing analysis are consistent with the results of previous investigations of this kind. The findings of this study, then, sustain the conclusion that the death penalty has little if anything to do with the relative occurrence of murder." [3]

We can go even further and point to the finding, which would appear quite paradoxical to a proponent of "the theory of deterrents," that in such states as Illinois, in which capital punishment does exist, the rate of homicides between 1931 and 1946, while fluctuating, maintained itself

[1] Charles Phillips, *Vacation Thoughts on Capital Punishment*, J. Ridgway, 1858.
[2] Karl F. Schuessler, "The Deterrent Influence of the Death Penalty." In *The Annals* of the American Academy of Political and Social Science, November, 1952, Vol. 284.
[3] *Ibid.*, p. 61.

on a level almost four times as high as the rate of homicides in the State of Wisconsin, which does not execute its murderers. Minnesota, which has no capital punishment, has an average of homicides two and one half times smaller than that of Colorado, which practices capital punishment, and roughly four times less than the rate in Oklahoma, Arizona, or New Mexico, which steadfastly keep on deterring in the old-fashioned way.

The problem is more complicated, of course, than my argument might make it appear. A number of factors—ethnic, general cultural, and perhaps economic—enter as determinants into the production of the phenomenon which is designated by the simple word "murder," or "homicide." It is not easy to isolate any one of these determinants and assess its role in the causation or inhibition of homicidal trends in a given society. However, capital punishment, being man-made, being introduced or abolished by man-made laws, stands out as an isolated factor; it appears to be both the most conspicuous and the most ineffectual of all the factors which appear to tend to inhibit man's propensity to kill his own kind.

If we now turn to the more personal, psychological aspects of the problem, we find rather general agreement as to the following among the psychological and sociological investigators of today: The man who is about to kill someone does not always, if ever, think of the consequences, still less of such a consequence as capital punishment. As a matter of fact, there seems to be a sort of indifference with regard to the consequences of the act, consequences which the criminal is supposed to know and the knowledge of which the prosecutor labors so hard to prove in each capital case.

The recent horrible murder of six-year-old Bobby Green-lease is one of the cases in point. Bonnie Brown Heady, the co-conspirator and co-author of the kidnaping and murder, and her partner in the crime, Carl Hall, showed little if any concern about what was ahead of them. Carl Hall was not deterred by his previous prison term for robbery from kidnaping and murdering an innocent little boy. As to Bonnie Brown Heady, she apparently knew what was ahead of her, but a possible death sentence did not deter her from assisting in the job of child killing. Hall, according to eyewitnesses, confessed to his crime and "sank into sullen silence," giving apparently no evidence of anxiety or despair. Bonnie Brown Heady made her confession to the police and then "asked for a pencil so she could work a crossword puzzle." "The request was refused because she was classed as a 'maximum security prisoner.' So she settled down with a comic book, *Intimate Love*." [4] Singular indifference indeed.

All this must be noted carefully, because various interpreters of crime utilize this indifference of criminals for various purposes, some of which are furthest removed from the goal of justice and from the principle of understanding crime. As a matter of fact, the revolting horror of a crime, the sickening feeling of fright and disgust such criminals arouse in us, make us even more convinced that their apparent indifference is but a sign of their callous incorrigibility and hopeless depravity, and that the only thing to do with them is to snuff them out.

This set of feelings is as frequent among people as it is natural, but it offers us no understanding of the event, it provides really no answer to the inevitable question: Why?

4 *Time*, October 19, 1953, p. 31.

This "why?" is uttered with desperation by the public, and the immediate answer is "Never mind, destroy the criminal, the human animal." This "why?" is uttered by the law in a tone of indignant objectivity, but actually it is but the echo of the hollow voice of "the man in the street" who, knowing nothing about human motives, "sees" the true answer only in the logic of acquiring easy money. This "why?" is asked by the sociologist, but his answer is but a number of statistics and generalizations, among which the person who committed the crime is lost, and with him the secret of the true answer. This "why?" is asked rather anxiously and almost desperately by the psychiatrist, but the world and/or the law offer him the obscurities of the McNaghten rule for a guide, or merely an electrocuted or hanged or gassed corpse. And corpses have no psychology; their answer is the silence of death. Or the psychiatrist may also be offered the "lifer," who is a ward of the state and is not allowed as a rule to be "pumped" by a psychiatrist.

Thus all the legitimate "whys?"—those of the desperate parents, of the frightened public, of the learned scientists and the administrators of the law—all remain a cry in the wilderness and a pitiful expression of self-confessed impotence which, however, is expressed in volumes of printed paper and many millions and millions of words. I, for one, do not feel at peace with this multivolumed and multivoiced impotence, and I do not wish entirely to bow to the desperation with which the public and the law seem to cling to the ancient principle of *lex talionis,* whether you call it retribution, or paying one's debt to society, or "serving one's time." Not that this desperation should be disregarded. First, it is a real desperation, fully justified by the facts of the given crime. And second, whatever method

may be considered most advisable, it is obvious that the
criminal must be set aside from the rest of us and treated
differently from the rest of us. He has a moral responsibility
to meet, a sin to expiate, and a job of self-rehabilitation to
perform with the help of the enlightened law and its administrators. Moreover, he has a sort of unwritten duty to
discharge—the duty to disclose the psychological secret
which is his as a criminal, and which he for the most part
does not know himself unless helped to learn and then to
teach us.

The pages that follow might perhaps help us to visualize
to some extent how all this might be achieved. But in the
meantime we must admit that the indifference of the criminal to the penalty that is ahead of him, even if this penalty
be death, is more the rule than the exception.

Lawes, the great warden of Sing Sing Prison in Ossining,
N. Y., and an opponent of capital punishment, saw one
hundred and fourteen people go to their legal deaths, and
he never was convinced that the criminal was ever deterred
by the knowledge or even the certainty that he was going
to be sentenced to death. Among the many instances cited,
here is one of the most telling. Writes Lawes:

Before Morris Wasser's execution, when I told him that the
governor had refused him a last-minute respite, he said bitterly:
"All right, Warden. It doesn't make much difference what I say
now about this here system of burning a guy, but I want to set you
straight on something."

"What's that?" I asked.

"Well, this electrocution business is the bunk. It don't do no
good, I tell you, and I know, because I never thought of the
chair when I plugged that old guy. And I'd probably do it again
if he had me on the wrong end of a rod."

"You mean," I said, "that you don't feel you've done wrong in taking another man's life?"

"No, Warden, it ain't that," he said impatiently. "I mean that you just don't think of the hot seat when you plug a guy. Somethin' inside you just makes you kill, 'cause you know, if you don't shut him up, it's curtains for you."

"I see. Then you never thought of what would happen to you at the time?"

"Hell, no! And lots of other guys in here, Harry, and Brick and Luke, all says the same thing. I tell you the hot seat will never stop a guy from pullin' a trigger."

"That was Wasser's theory," concludes Warden Lawes, "and I've heard it echoed many times since." [5]

I do not assume for the moment that these arguments and considerations close once and for all the discussion as to the deterrent value of the death penalty or any other form of harsh punishment. There is a great deal of psychological tension and emotional power behind the traditional belief in deterrents, and more than mere argumentation is required to settle the question. However, I hope it has become clear that without psychological insight (and deep insight) into the workings of the mind of the criminal, the question in question can never be settled.

[5] Warden Lewis E. Lawes, *Meet the Murderer!* Harper, 1940, pp. 178-79.

3.

SOME DIFFERENCES IN
PROFESSIONAL PSYCHOLOGY

WE THUS reach, perhaps, the greatest impasse of the problem under discussion, a most threatening one and a most difficult one to negotiate. It is like an immense canyon, the sharp edges of whose brim seem to make it impossible to attach a rope which might be thrown to the other side. The circumference seems immense, so that one cannot hope that it may ever be covered on foot or otherwise. The problem is how to bridge this chasm, how to bring together those two voices which are heard from either side, at times appealing to one another, at times cursing one another. I have in mind the law and medical psychology.

I have no easy or direct answer as to how to bridge this canyon, this gap, and I don't want to join the somewhat traditional chorus of voices which lull those interested with the assurance that the gap is already being closed. In my opinion we have not reached the stage of understanding even some of the elementary aspects of our respective languages. We have not gone beyond the stage of recognizing that we occupy different positions on opposite sides of the canyon, and the hope that we might some day bridge the gap.

If we are truly to bridge the gap, what will be of help to us? I think first of deep curiosity about the understanding of the criminal by both medical psychology and the law, and consequently of fundamental and radical, extensive reform of our punitive system and the system of rehabilitation of the transgressor of the law. In this connection it is almost as important to set forth what I do not have in mind, or considerable confusion will inevitably ensue. What I do not have in mind is the service medical psychology might render the law in the business of detecting crime, bringing the criminal to trial, and punishing him. Whenever a criminological problem is under discussion, I endeavor to make it clear that in the business of helping the law psychiatry, like toxicology or general physiological and organic chemistry, can be used by the law only as a valuable adjuvant for the work of the police, prosecuting attorney, and judge. But this particular brand of psychiatry is medical only to the extent that the people who do the job are medical men, or guided by the latter. To be medical in the true sense of the word we must consider the curative, restorative, correctional aspects of medicine, and view them as inseparable from the total concept of medical psychology, or psychiatry.

This said, we find ourselves at a crossroads. At the point of crossing stand both law and psychiatry, but as they begin to move they start moving apart. Why? A lead to the right answer might be found in an excerpt from a letter of Harold Laski to Justice Holmes. You will recall the excerpt from the letter of Justice Holmes in which he likened the criminal to be executed to a soldier dying for his country—but with dishonor, of course. That was in part in response to Laski, who had written to Holmes about a fortnight before. Said Laski:

Since I wrote last week I think the most interesting thing I have done was to take the chair at a discussion of a philosophical society on Criminal Responsibility. The protagonists were Travers Humphreys, one of our best criminal lawyers, and a Dr. Hyslop, a great mental specialist. There was no doubt in my mind that the lawyer had the best of it. The medicals spoke passionately of "uncontrollable impulses" and such like; Humphreys always drove them back to the vital point of getting definitions which could be explained by a judge to an average jury, and I thought he showed admirably that the refinements of psychological analysis are not yet ripe for legal use.[1]

This was written on December 1, 1925; it could easily have been written in January, 1954, with the same authority and prestige, with the same power of conviction and of convincing the average man, with the same prejudice against psychiatry and the same lack of understanding of the basic issues involved.

First, no average (or superior) jury understands the complex chemistry involving the detection of stains of human blood. Nor does any jury understand the niceties of titration or other methods used to detect traces of a given poison in a given organ. But the chemist testifies, and the jury accepts his findings as facts. No jury has the slightest understanding of the processes and techniques involved in dissecting carefully such an organ as, say, the stomach, and separating it accurately from the intestine, or separating the duodenum from the transverse colon. The jury may be shown some sort of grayish, slimy-looking, frayed and snaky something in a jar filled with some preservative, or rather, ill-smelling fluid—for the jury will easily perceive the smell, but whether it is a preservative fluid or something else the jury will not know. But the jury will believe that it is a preservative fluid containing a piece of intestine through

[1] *Holmes-Laski Letters,* pp. 804-05.

which a bullet passed causing inflammation, etc. The jury will take a great deal on faith in such matters, and so will more than one enlightened jurist. But the medical psychologist cannot put his findings in Formalin or Zenker's solution and parade them for the jury to smell and see and believe with all the faith into which the human eye can mislead.

Shall the whole business of psychological analysis then be dropped? As if to say: no jars, no solutions—then no psychology and no further understanding are required or even possible. Before such a definitive rejection even tempts a Travers Humphreys, one ought to cast a glance on what the criminal lawyer insists. He insists on *getting definitions* which the judge would then take and redefine to the jury in some language which an average jury could understand.

It is common knowledge, of course, how recondite and diffuse psychiatrists can be, and how little sense they convey to thinking men or to themselves when they try to shoot holes into the armor of the law with the paper wads of psychiatric jargon. If the opponents of psychological analysis have only this in mind, they are right, of course. But they are also infinitely wrong, because they do not see the imposing edifice of truly scientific psychopathology for the paper wads of psychologizing contentions, with which latter so many people identify the whole discipline of medical psychology.

Without going into the deeper motivations right now, it must be admitted that there seems to exist a deep antagonism between psychiatry and the law. Well, antagonism is a "big" word which the average jury might misunderstand. I shall not sin against the meaning of the word as it is used here if I say that antagonism means or generates unfriendly tension; well, again "tension" might be too big a word for the average jury, so let me say instead "unfriendly discomfort," or still better and more simply, "mutual dislike," or still more simply, "hostility." Yes, "hostility," not "simple dislike," because only when one is hostile does one want to shoot full of holes what the other fellow has to say. This hostility between psychiatry and the law is actually being displayed every day in front of juries, and the act can be fairly described as a display of mutual hostility no matter who gets the better of whom. This display the jury sees; this the jury understands. The jury does not know why it is so; the jury does not know where the hostility comes from (although it also dislikes "that psychology business"). Let us not dwell on the obvious any longer and merely say (in the language of the psychopathologist, of course): This obvious hostility between psychiatry and the law is but a reflection of the universal antagonism with which humanity is burdened. When it is not manifest, it is not dead or otherwise nonexistent, it merely seethes under the surface until it becomes manifest. In other words, it is always there, and it comes out more easily than we would like; we make attempts to conceal it, but we do so with considerable awkwardness and almost always with bad grace. The hostility is there. We usually call it aggression. It is protean in its manifestations, and omnipresent. You will find it on the golf course and in the murderer's den; you will find it in the courtroom and in the street fight between a couple of urchins. It is a universal property of man. It is also universally manifest, particularly if you are trained to make psychological observations.

In order to gain some understanding of this baffling property of man, we shall have to study a number of things; and for our purposes it is necessary first to gain some understanding as to what happens to the lawyer and the psychiatrist respectively with regard to this property called aggression. What happens to the future lawyer and the future psychiatrist from the time their training starts?

Harold Laski admired Travers Humphreys for driving "back to the vital point of getting definitions." In this statement it is almost easy to find a clue to the solution of the whole problem. The lawyer begins his training with definitions—direct, crisp, clear-cut, so-called "self-understood" definitions. With definitions—which means with predetermined theoretical categories made into principles—the lawyer proceeds to test individual and social life from the standpoint of whether or not these fit into those categories. There is little freedom in the law except for the rare authoritative interpreter, and even the latter is bound by precedent, by *stare decisis,* by categories properly defined in advance. This principle the lawyer learns early, as he learns early to be on the lookout for those who violate the well-defined, established law. If a given law happens to be not very well defined, it stands as such until better defined and it is applied in the meantime in the best possible manner.

The doctor from the very beginning finds himself surrounded with mysteries which defy definition, or thoroughly baffle him at any rate. His first encounter with medicine is the meeting with death in the dissecting room; he starts his medical studies in the stench of death, among corpses and not among the living. Thus the first thing he is reminded of when he enters medical school is that he will die the way all these other people on the tables have died, that he too will decompose the way all these other people have done or are doing or are going to do. The future doctor then

turns to the skeleton and studies the bones of man denuded
of living human flesh and hollowed out without live marrow
or brain, and the future doctor learns to know that he too
has such bones, and that they will some day become just as
denuded and hollow. And then the future doctor, when
he begins his analytical work in chemistry, makes analyses
of urine and of feces, and of his own urine and his own
feces; and it is a common joke, a universal theme for laugh-
ter, when the beginner tries to suck up in a pipette a small
and definite amount of urine, and inevitably overshoots the
mark now and then and finds his mouth full of urine.

Unpleasant and funny all this, but it is quite impressive
that from the very first day the future doctor is confronted
with a very striking psychological situation. He learns that
he too will be as dead as the corpse he learns to dissect; that
his own urine may contain foreign matter; that his own
blood may contain the plasmodium of malaria; that his
own feces may contain the amoeba of dysentery; that he
too may have tuberculosis, a tumor of the brain, infantile
paralysis, a cancer of the stomach, a broken leg or a pul-
monary hemorrhage. In other words, from the very outset
the young doctor is taught, and he must learn to feel or to
know how others feel, the various pains and aches and dis-
solutions of life, the deformities and enormities of illness,
the finality of death.

For the rest of his professional career the doctor will deal
with the people he was taught to see and feel for and with,
the people with whom he was taught to identify himself,
as the technical psychological language puts it.

Imagine a lawyer learning to see and to feel everything
his clients, or the defendants who will appear before him,
will see and feel. The young doctor experiences himself

many of the things he learns. He is in direct contact with the sick and he, as a student, has sought to determine the action of certain drugs by trying them on himself. Later on, as a doctor, he does not consider it out of the ordinary if someone in the profession exposes himself to a given illness, thus contracts it, and thus learns and teaches. Imagine a lawyer making it a prerequisite part of his training to be a pickpocket, a thief, an embezzler, a kidnaper, a murderer, and then coming back after he had been imprisoned or executed to be graduated with honors as a true criminal lawyer.

I do not want anyone to think for a moment that this is my considered advice as a psychiatrist as to the vocational training of a jurist; I am fully aware that I myself did not go through a schizophrenia, agoraphobia, depression, and suicide to come back to graduate as a psychopathologist.

However, the conclusion imposes itself that the lawyer (for our purposes, the criminal lawyer) is taught emotionally, sociologically, and professionally to be estranged from the people who will become his major concern as a judge or prosecutor or defense counsel. By the same token, the conclusion imposes itself that the physician is taught to become emotionally, sociologically, and professionally one with the people and the medical conditions which are to become his chief professional concern.

This is the first great psychological gap between the two professions.

I sometimes think how wonderful the effect on legal education would be to have a more human contact between the future lawyer and those with whom he will have to deal later. What would happen, for instance, if young law students included in their studies visits to jails and prisons, and served as prison guards for a while, the way medical students serve as clerks in hospitals during their student days; if the young law student were required to attend so many executions, as medical students are required to attend and report on so many autopsies; if the law student got some authentic case histories from various prisoners and compared them with their court and probation-officer records, in the same manner as medical students and interns are required to take case histories and examine patients and then compare the data thus obtained with the hospital records?

I do not think there would be anything wrong or illegal if a law student and young lawyer had all these experiences, and thus learned through actual experience what people are and what they are like as compared with the colorless, impersonal descriptions as the law presents them. The lawyer, armed with such experience, would not then have to rely on his own prejudices, which are ingrained in him by the economic group, cultural class, or special family conditions from which he happens to come. He would find himself less estranged from people as they actually are and not as the definitions say they are. And he would also find himself closer to the doctor.

For the whole background of the doctor, from the dissecting room through the hospital ward to the autopsy room, is that of a uniquely co-ordinated training in combating not the people he deals with but that which is the matter with them. Imagine a lawyer with the same psychological orientation. I do not mean by this that the lawyer should become a psychologist in his own right. I mean rather that his own psychology as a professional man might be such that he would not tend to combat and eliminate people as if he were the sanitary tool of some super-socio-logical housecleaning department. Rather, he would (in conformity with the law to be sure) try to dispose of people in such a manner that the people would be preserved and rehabilitated in their totality—that only the inner or outer conditions of which they had become victims would be abolished.

One can think along such lines *without* considering every crime the product of some disease, for such a point of view would be extremely erroneous: not every criminal is ill, not every crime is a result of psychological pathology. I will not tire of repeating this, because so many people fail to understand that the sociological principle of rehabilitation of the delinquent, while requiring a great deal of psychological knowledge, does not mean in any way that every delinquent act is a psychopathological act.

However, let us return to our principal problem. The point I wish to make here, or to emphasize particularly, is this.

Every profession has its psychology. Every professional educational system bears the earmarks of this psychology. Furthermore, a medical education tends to direct all the aggressive capacity of the doctor against the afflictions from which the patients suffer, not against the object of the doctor's primary concern—his patient. The lawyer, on the other hand, is taught to stand up against the violator as well as the violation of the law. This is true especially of criminal law. Even a lawyer for the defense is tinged with this social hostility, which the criminal law teaches him as apparently it must. It is only very rarely that a great lawyer is able to rise above this professional hostility.

This professional hostility as well as the hostility between the professions of law and psychiatry would, I believe, diminish considerably and ultimately disappear, if both the lawyer and the psychiatrist could meet at the crossroads and make the crossroads common ground at least as far as two points are concerned.

Point one: The human personality is not a static category of unshakable logic, but an indivisible totality which is in constant motion and commotion. It is outside the scope of this book to dwell on this particular aspect of human psychology, but I think of one experiment which might prove highly instructive in this connection. If young lawyers were afforded the opportunity to have so-called "lie detector" or "narco-analytic" interviews with mentally healthy and mentally ill people, such interviews to be conducted jointly with an experienced psychiatrist, it would at once become apparent to both doctor and lawyer what is meant by "alteration of personality," as well as its indivisible unity. They would both at one and the same time be able to observe the frailty and illogical unity that is man, something that transgresses formalistic definitions.

Point two: Both the lawyer and the psychiatrist must have a clear conception of human aggression—conscious and unconscious. Without a clear understanding of this problem in human psychology, you can neither cure the psychologically ill nor justly punish or rehabilitate the criminal.

Without a true understanding of the varieties and vicissitudes of human aggression, there can be no true understanding of the criminal act—and I have in mind, of course, both psychological and legal understanding.

4.

AGGRESSION AND TRANSGRESSION

Thus far, we have dealt with general principles more or less, and have cited an example here and there which was rather extreme, more or less. I say this not by way of apology but rather by way of reminding the reader that I did not promise to take the middle ground wherever in my opinion no middle ground exists. Sometimes it is only from examples which appear extreme that we can learn the real meaning of what a given phenomenon is. It is only when we look into a miscroscope through a lens of high power that we are able to recognize certain bacteria which otherwise would entirely escape our purview.

Take as an example the vexing questions of responsibility for a given crime as the law sees it. It is impossible to observe and objectively to establish at which point of mental functioning the law would stop and say: until now, up to this point, the accused was irresponsible, and from now on he begins to be responsible. This is the reason why the law itself deals either in such extremes as its own nonclinical definition of a condition it calls insanity, or in artificial, purely verbal delineations of greater or lesser responsibility.

All this is very discouraging indeed. But it was borne upon me with a sense of particular impact how discouraging the problem of crime and the criminal is when I came upon a little volume called *Rationale of Crime and Its Ap-*

*propriate Treatment, Being a Treatise on Criminal Juris-
prudence Considered in Relation to Cerebral Organization.*
This little work was written by one M. B. Sampson, and it
first appeared in installments in the *Spectator* in London,
in 1838. The second edition was republished in America,
in New York and Philadelphia, in 1846, "with notes and
illustrations by E. W. Farnham, Matron of Mount Pleasant
State Prison," which was in New York and apparently what
is now the Women's Prison in Bedford Hills, N. Y. Matron
Farnham states in her introductory preface: ". . . To adapt
[this treatise] somewhat more perfectly to the purpose of
interesting the popular mind—for it is emphatically on the
popular mind in republican America that such a work must
exert its chief influence—the editor has added some of the
many facts which her own experience and that of others
have furnished, illustrative of its most novel doctrines." [1]

These "novel doctrines" were no other than the theory
of Gall's phrenology, which had seen its day over seventy-
five years ago. Yet there is something of great even though
melancholy interest, and something discouragingly reveal-
ing, in this little book. The author and its editor are profound believers in phrenology and the complex fantasy of
cerebral localization which it represented. With enthusiasm
and hope the author points out how it became possible to
view crime and the criminal in the light of a new and great
truth about human psychology and behavior. He thinks
about the fact that fifty years before he set his pen to writing his book, and before the trustees of "The Henderson
Fund for the Advancement of Phrenology" had resolved
upon the publication of it, it would have been impossible
to view crime and the criminal with such clarity, such in-

[1] P. xiii.

sight and humanitarian understanding! It does seem more than a little quaint to read all this and recall how we today, referring to Freud and psychoanalysis, say that fifty years ago it would have been impossible for us to understand the act of the criminal as we do in the light of the deeper psychology of today, and how now we are on the threshold of a new change in our attitude toward criminological problems.

Over a hundred years have passed since Sampson made his passionate appeal for a better understanding of criminal "impulses, desires, and acts which . . . [heretofore] set both reason and charity at defiance, when these could examine only external causes and circumstances, [but which] are now clearly explicable by reference to the existence and force of internal causes." [2] These are the words of Matron Farnham, ten years before Freud was born. Inspiring and discouraging words they are—and even more so if we take into consideration the various objections which are raised against the "novel doctrines" of today. The objections are strikingly similar to those of one hundred and fifteen years ago. I cannot express my own thoughts better than by using the words of Mr. Sampson, the author of the *Rationale of Crime:*

. . . it is probable that my readers will suggest the following objections:

(1) That the doctrine which I now advocate would destroy all ideas of responsibility.

(2) That it would leave all men to follow their inclinations with impunity; and,

(3) That, as it would enforce no punishment on offenders, it would present nothing that could deter others from following their example.[3]

[2] P. xv.
[3] P. 44.

I cannot refrain from responding in part to the above, again with the words of the same writer:

The doctrine of responsibility, which appears to me to be alone consistent with reason, religion, and morality, is simply this: that, so far from the Creator having sent into the world some beings who are responsible, and others who are exempt from responsibility, there is, in fact, no exception whatever; and that every human being is alike responsible,—responsible . . . to undergo the painful but benevolent treatment which is requisite for his cure.[4]

With these warnings to possible objectors of traditional cast, let us for a moment consider a criminal act, any criminal act, any transgression, from the standpoint of what appears to move the transgressor. No one would object to the statement that the transgressor seems to be moved by ill-will. "Ill-will" in the common, conversational sense means a desire, a wish to do harm; there is ill-will whether we are dealing with a pickpocket, a kleptomaniac, an impulsive murderer, or premeditated, well-planned assassination.

The reader will at once notice that I seem to avoid the distinction between conscious ill-will (pickpocket, premeditated murder) and unconscious ill-will (kleptomania, impulsive homicide). I avoid the differentiation between conscious and unconscious "will" or drive because I wish for a moment to focus attention on the meaning of the criminal act itself. The criminal act does some injury to someone. It is an act of aggression. I would avoid the usual emphasis that a criminal act is antisocial. Of course, it is an antisocial act, but from the standpoint of the criminal, acting for conscious or unconscious reasons, he acts not because his inner

4 P. 50.

motivation is antisocial and rebellious against the laws of the land, but because he feels (or unconsciously experiences) a desire to do injury, or enhance his own sense of power, by depriving someone of pocket money or life.

This desire, this need is a hostility, aggressively acted out. Present-day psychology views this quality, this inner drive, this set of inner impulses, as a special instinctual drive and gives it the generic name of aggression. Its presence in man is universal and protean. It lives with us and within us from birth till we die. It is an ingredient of everything that is good as well as evil in our behavior. The man who takes life "lying down," which means without a certain amount of aggression like self-assertion, creative effort, initiative, and originality, does not really live; he may continue to exist, but it is an existence more vegetable than human. This is like the existence we begin with, when we are babies; but even at the moment of our birth, the first cry we emit with the first breath we take in is already an expression of protest, *i.e.*, an aggressive response. From our first cry on, helpless though we are at the outset, we accumulate within us quantities of aggressive drives. And as we go on in life we are confronted with the gigantic task of what is in our psychological jargon called "handling our aggression." Very soon we learn that our loud voices and our banging on the floor for fun are not always welcome; very soon we learn that we must hold in check our exuberances and our combative effervescence.

Two observations must be made in this connection:

(1) A repressed aggressive drive, that is to say, an aggressive drive inhibited and rendered unconscious, does not disappear; it merely becomes invisible to the outside world

and "unthinkable" to the person in whose unconscious this aggression dwells.

(2) This aggression rendered unconscious gets a free sway in the unconscious; it weaves its fantasies with imaginative lack of restraint, and it causes considerable anxiety and a sense of guilt conscious and unconscious. A severe sense of guilt can exist in the absence of one single overt act of hostility. A sense of guilt means a self-reproaching attitude, a self-accusatory one, a self-attacking one, an attitude of being aggressive against one's own self. This is a universal phenomenon common to all of us. In its severer pathological form it may lead to suicide, which does seem to justify the older appellation of self-homicide, or felony of one's own self.

It would seem then that if too great an amount of aggression is turned inward, as the saying goes, we may have to do with a suicide; if it is turned outward, we may deal with a murder. Many sociological writers were wont to point out in pre-Freudian days that in certain parts of the world, or even in certain provinces of the same country, the average number of suicides and homicides stands in some inverse relationship. This observation would bear out the psychoanalytic views on the dynamics of aggression. The comparative diminution of the number of suicides in times of war would suggest that the civil population lives out a great deal of hostility vicariously in times of war, and consequently there is less aggression turned inward—for in wartime it is permitted to hate and to count the number of the killed in the enemy camp with a certain sense of triumph. Perhaps the increase in crimes in the time immediately following the end of wars is due to the immense amount of aggression, liberated but not lived out or stopped by the mere act of an armistice or peace treaty.

While all this may sound simple and almost mechanical, it is neither mechanical nor simple. Yet it is all quite mysterious; for the apparent psychological difference between the man who commits suicide and the man who commits murder (impulsive or otherwise) seems to be only the direction which the destructive hostility takes. If it is turned against the person himself, he is a suicide; if it is directed against another person, it is murder.

Would it were so simple. What happens psychologically is this: before they are ready to come out in the form of real action—suicidal, or homicidal, or some equivalent of both or either—the aggressive drives within us live their own life as it were, a life of most elaborate unconscious presentations and imagery. There are fantasies of biting and tearing and cutting and tormenting, and fantasies of being bitten and torn and cut and tormented. These fantasies are not limited to neurotic and psychotic individuals; they become more manifest in neuroses and psychoses, but they are present in us all. They may reach a considerable richness of elaboration and emotional intensity. They may even enter consciousness, and yet not lead to any action, not even to anxiety. They may go on for years and occupy a considerable part of a man's daydreaming life, or fill his nightmares, and yet not make him break out into action—the technical term is "acting out" one's forbidden fantasies.

The mysterious thing about the whole matter is that there seems to be as yet no satisfactory explanation of why certain individuals start *acting out* their fantasy life either in the form of annoying neurotic social behavior, or in the form of criminal acts. Psychoanalysis has uncovered a wealth of clinical data enriching our understanding of the deeper psychology of the normal, the neurotic, and the psychotic, whether he be criminal or not. But it has no answer as to what it is that makes man succumb or give in to his fantasies so that they become criminal acts.

What we see in the courts and in prisons are only a few examples of those specimens of humanity who fell victim or gave in to the pressure of their fantasies and impulses. There are innumerable similar instances in daily life, seen particularly by the practicing psychopathologist—instances of transitional states, quasi-criminal and nearly acted out transgressions of which the law will never know. And there are instances of painful inner struggles against near-acting out, or of attempts to conceal from the outside world that which the given persons really want, think, plan, and do to a certain extent. These instances cover the whole gamut of human perversity, moral and social; the name of the variations is legion, and the degrees of perversity innumerable. So imperceptibly do they blend one into another that no clear-cut definitions, no crisp, succinct descriptions are possible.

There is the respectable businessman who goes into a store, tries on a suit, and walks out with it without paying for it, never to return to the store, never to be caught, and leading a respectable, honest family life. There are sexual perverts who indulge in sadistic and masochistic practices which are never discovered by the law. There are people who steal from their neighbors and, never discovered, continue to visit them and play bridge with them. And there are instances of more serious actions, including murder.

When an unconscious fantasy breaks out into consciousness and stays there on the same basis as it had lived previously in the unconscious, the individual in question will tell you, or think to himself, of these fantasies, sometimes mistaking them for facts; then these fantasies become delusions. Why certain delusions continue to remain delusions and others are acted out in behavior, the present-day psychopathologist is unable to answer. But this much he does know: these fantasies, whether they remain unconscious, or break out into consciousness and are perceived as horrifying, painful foreign bodies to the self of the person who has them, or enter consciousness seemingly emaciated, as it were, as if devoid of any emotional accompaniment at all—these fantasies, regardless of their state, form, or emotional appearance, have somewhere a pleasurable meaning to the person who is their bearer or victim; and this pleasurable meaning is more often than not connected with some kind of sexual overtone, or actually sexual feeling.

It requires a great deal of careful study and considerable experience in dealing with the unconscious to detect these elements in milder cases, or to bring them out into the open for others to notice. It is here that the present-day psychiatrist meets with the greatest difficulties in the exercise of his professional duties. The average man of the jury demands that the psychiatrist be simple and rational, that he make his demonstrations tangible, fitting the mold of formal thinking. The trouble is that this is very difficult to do. The medical psychologist has no instruments by means of which he can measure the degree of unconscious hate, the weight of charity or conscience, the kilogram-meters of will power.

The medical psychologist is a clinician who deals with a special kind of material which is called psychological; his work can be likened to that of putting together a jigsaw puzzle. If all the pieces of a jigsaw puzzle fit and make a picture, the right solution has been found. No amount of logic could explain why this or that piece of a jigsaw puzzle is half round or cut in the form of a question mark or of an irregular triangle, but altogether they make the picture, say, of "Washington Crossing the Delaware," and no other picture can be concocted from the pieces at hand.

In medical psychology the work is much the same. It is tedious work; at times one does not know where one is going, but gradually the work of fitting pieces together, of proper reconstruction is done. All this is not in the manner of traditional science; but it is accurate, true in its results, and there is no arbitrariness about it. No matter how much we may try to imitate the modes and procedures of modern scientific instrumentation, we shall never be able to attain the intimate understanding of a given individual without a jigsaw method of reconstructing this given individual's psychological totality, his picture in action, as it were.

The nonpsychiatrist must bear in mind this essential methodological difference between the psychiatrist's clinical evaluation of a case, and the physicist's or physiologist's or any other purely scientific worker's.

It is only through the method of jigsaw reconstruction, for instance, that the inefficacy of executive clemency in certain cases can be proved. I recall the case of an intellectual worker who killed a farmer under rather strange circumstances. He was tried, convicted to life imprisonment, and after a comparatively short period was pardoned. He left the state in which he had been imprisoned, and moved far away to a large industrial and academic center, where he made a new life and a new career for himself. No one there knew of his past. But the more smoothly successful his life became, the more moody and self-derogatory he grew. Finally, after more than a decade had elapsed since the tragedy of murder occurred, he could stand it no longer and made a rather brutal attempt to mutilate himself (castrate himself with a razor). He was prevented from carrying out his intention and placed in a mental hospital where he sat brooding, eyes closed, as if shutting out the world. He gradually revealed his past, which was verified and confirmed.

This also is one of the extreme and therefore telling examples of how a sense of guilt (despite the debt paid by a prison term) can remain and germinate within the psychic apparatus, grow to the point of becoming intolerable, and ultimately, through his own pathological conscience, make the bearer of the sense of guilt his own executioner. The point of special interest in this case is that the sense of guilt has gone beyond the demands of legal justice. There are transgressors of the law who kill to die (cf. above, Maudsley's case of Burton), and if the law fails to kill them, they find their own way to death.

The law seldom sees such cases, for they usually kill themselves on the spot. On the other hand, in cases of suicide pacts where one party survives, the accidental survivor must stand trial for murder, and he not infrequently presents a strong suicidal trend which the law cannot quench. Or, by way of psychotic denial of the whole act, the shot turned against one's self is forgotten or elaborated into a complicated delusion in accordance with which someone else came and attacked; the truth is forgotten, delusion takes its place, and the prisoner serves his long prison sentence with bitter complaints, with an acrid sense of injustice done because the allegedly real culprit is somewhere at large while he, the prisoner, is an innocent victim with a bullet in his head, "rotting in this joint." He will show you X rays of his skull, he will tell you his medical history. His aggression, his hostility is now turned against the alleged miscarriage of justice, of which he keeps on repetitively reciting the events like an old phonograph record. The law does not deter such a man from anything, not even from his delusionary psychosis; but it does seem to serve the purpose of giving the derelict an object to hate: the prison, its bars, its existence. Consequently, such men do not attempt to kill themselves.

Occasionally we find a specimen of criminal humanity which is not so circumscribed, and is so abundant in detail and so striking that it looks like a museum for psychopathological demonstrations. Such a case was that of Fish, who at the age of sixty-five was executed by the State of New York some years ago for the murder of a little girl.

Fish was known as Albert Fish, although Albert was not his given name. Fish appropriated it when his brother died. Fish at the time was fourteen years old; in other words, he had approximately reached puberty. Fish was the youngest of seven by a second marriage. His father was a sea captain, naturally interested in ships and the sea. Fish's father died when the boy was five years old—a uniquely precarious age from the point of view of psychosexual development. He was cared for in an orphanage for two years, and then by a widow who had a crippled daughter. Fish's Sunday-school teacher had reasons to hope that some day he would enter the ministry. He enjoyed reading the Bible; his other favorite books were those describing the torture of the early Christians, and those about the Spanish Inquisition.

By profession Fish was a house painter. He was married,

and after he had raised a sizable family his wife left him. One of his daughters became the real head of the family. Fish led a very religious life, and for approximately eleven years he was both father and mother to his family. He was never known to have punished any of his children. He was always gentle, kind, warmhearted, loving, and very solicitous.

It was disclosed that despite this very kind appearance and behavior he liked to torture himself. He used to stick long needles into his perineum, lower abdomen, and buttocks and leave them in until they became covered with skin. When Fish was arrested, an X-ray photograph revealed the presence of thirty needles in his body. He thought he had stuck the needles into himself because a message from Christ made him do it. He invented what he called a paddle, a sort of little brush with nails, and he loved to spank himself with it. Sometimes he asked others to spank him with this paddle.

He was fifty-seven years old when he killed a little girl, but one year before while working in St. Louis as a house painter he once caught a Negro boy and tortured him for several days in a cellar, and made an attempt to cut off the boy's genitals.

Fish's daughter related that her father used to eat his meat almost raw, or not cooked at all. This was his favorite food, and his favorite drink was sweet cider. He liked peanut butter. When asked what he liked most he answered: carrots, frankfurters, and a switch. He was frankly and openly coprophilic.

For many years he had a very gruesome cannibalistic fantasy of which the reader will learn presently. He wrote many letters to many people about this fantasy, as if it were a true fact.

Some weeks before the crime was committed, Fish bought a butcher knife, a cleaver, and a saw, wrapped these up in a neat package and left the package at a newsstand near an elevated station where he was known. He had no particular thought or plans at the time.

While awaiting death in prison he cried a little when he spoke about his wife's having left him years ago, or about the murder. During the rest of the time he remained totally dull and unresponsive. He succeeded in corroding the corner of a table and would rub his abdomen against that corroded corner till he bled. All the time he would murmur to himself. It was definitely observed and admitted that he derived complete sexual gratification in this manner.

In response to a newspaper advertisement telling of a young man wanting a job, Fish went to the house of the young man. The latter was not at home. Fish appeared very kind and pleasant; he told a lie, representing himself as an affluent truck farmer from Long Island. He said he would come again, that he was not in a hurry to fill the position. While he was talking he noticed a little girl, the sister of the man who was looking for a job. He quickly made friends with her. He gave her some candies. She sat on his lap. Fish said his sister was giving a party next Sunday, and he would like to take the little girl to that party. The impression made by Fish was that of such an honest and good man that next Sunday when he arrived the child was already dressed in party clothes, waiting for him.

When he came to the little girl's house he confessed later that "I sort of had a feeling come across me to take the little girl instead of the boy," and it is quite striking to learn that during the act of killing the girl he thought she was a boy.

On the way to the "party" Fish stopped and picked up the butcher tools which had been kept for him in a package at the newsstand. Then he and the girl took a train; they got off the train somewhere in Westchester County. The girl noticed that Fish had forgotten the package, and she rushed back and brought it to him. With these tools she was murdered and dismembered.

Why did Fish kill Grace Budd? Well, that day when he first saw her the first thought that occurred to him was that she would be raped some day; he decided then and there to save her from the tragic shame. He considered it his mission to have her die a virgin. He thought at the same time that he was Abraham sacrificing his son Isaac.

Please note how devilishly interlaced are here idealized virginity and confusion of sexes, or rather, alternation of sex objects, as if there was an alternation of homosexual and heterosexual pedophilic drives. The wish to attack sexually appears as a desire to protect from rape. The brutality of animal impulses is perceived as a quasi-religious missionary exaltation.

It is rather telling that, having committed the murder, Albert Fish, while seemingly continuing his usual life, did seem to begin to seek quite unconsciously, I am sure, some sort of punishment at the hands of the law. Within a few months he was arrested three times for some minor offenses and set free. A year before the murder he married illegally; and he married twice again illegally two years later. He started sending out obscene letters in pursuance of an old habit, and he was apprehended; the judge this time was more discerning than the psychiatrist. The judge sent Fish to a mental hospital. The mental hospital notified the court that examinations and tests revealed nothing criminal, nothing homicidal or suicidal in the man, but that he gave evidence of early stages of senile dementia. Fish was set free again.

His unconscious play with the fire of the law had not even singed him. Fish continued his psychologically precarious meandering in this queerly healthy world of ours, in the largest metropolis of the world, unsuspected and unmolested. It seems that finally his unconscious conscience could no longer bear to live with the ambiguities of his own strange mind, and he finally wrote a letter to his little victim's mother. The letter revealed his lifelong fantasy about a sea captain (his father had been one), and about cannibalism, and it also told the story of the murder, which story was later on confirmed in detail and the *corpus delicti* established.

My dear Mrs. Budd:

In 1894 a friend of mine shipped as a deck-hand on the steamer Tacoma, Captain Davis. They sailed from San Francisco for Hong Kong, China. On arriving there he and two others went ashore and got drunk. When they returned the boat was gone. At that time there was a famine in China. Meat of any kind [that is underscored] was from one dollar to three dollars a pound. So great was the suffering among the very poor that all children under twelve years were sold to the butchers to be cut up and sold for food in order to keep others from starving. A boy or girl under fourteen was not safe in the street. You could go in any shop and ask for steak, chops or stew meat. Part of the naked body of a boy or girl would be brought out and just what you wanted cut from it. A boy or girl's behind, which is the sweetest part of the body and sold as veal cutlet, brought the highest price. John stayed there so long he acquired a taste for human flesh. On his return to New York he stole two boys, one seven, one eleven, took them to his home, stripped them naked, tied them in a closet, then burned everything they had on. Several times every day and night he spanked them, tortured them, to make their meat good and tender. First he killed the eleven-year-old boy because he had the fattest [behind] and of course the most meat on it. Every part of his body was cooked and eaten, except head, bones and guts, he roasted in the oven. All of his [behind] boiled, broiled, fried, stewed. The little boy was next, went the same way. At this time I was living at 409 East 100th Street, rear right side. He told me so often how good flesh was, I made up my mind to taste it. On Sunday, June 3, 1928, I called on you at 406 West 15th Street, brought you pot cheese—strawberries. We had lunch. Grace sat on my lap and kissed me. I made up my mind to eat her, on the pretext of taking her to a party. You said yes she could go. I took her to an empty house in Westchester I had already picked out. When we got there I told her to remain outside. She picked wild flowers. I went upstairs and stripped all of my clothes off. I knew if I did not I would get her blood on them. When all was ready I went to the window and called her. Then I hid in a closet until she was in the room. When she saw me all naked she began to cry and tried to run downstairs. I grabbed her, and she said she would tell her mamma. First I stripped her naked. How she did kick and bite and scratch. I choked her to death, then cut her in small pieces so I could take the meat to my rooms, cook it and eat it. Her sweet and tender little [behind] was roasted in the oven. It took me nine days to eat her entire body. I did not have [intercourse] with her although I could have had I wished. She died a virgin.

The letter was produced in court by the defense and it is a part of the printed record of the trial. What is noteworthy in this whole gruesome story is that the act of killing the child seemed psychologically less important to Fish than the gustatory cannibalistic gratification he experienced. It is worth noting in addition that in relating the whole story there is no display of regret, but rather a sense of pious reassurance that the child died a virgin, also, that this letter, which was in fact a confession and was traced to Fish and led to his arrest, was offered to the mother of the victim as a consolation, as a bit of solace: "She died a virgin." There is no trace of human understanding of how a mother would feel in reading the cannibalistic story of her own baby's being choked to death, cut to pieces and devoured. There is perhaps more than a tinge of the need to torment the poor mother with all these horrible details. Perhaps Fish in writing this letter re-experienced the same spasmodic sexual gratification which, as it was established, he experienced twice during the strangely quasi-ritualistic act of murder.

Let me avoid here, as I have until now, the use of highly technical psychological terms. I continue to refrain from using these terms as much as is humanly possible, in order thus to demonstrate that complex psychological reactions can be stated and described in strictly human terms and therefore can be understood easily by court and jury. To be sure, a strictly scientific account of a case would require the use of the scientific terminology. It is my conviction, however, that psychological terminology today all too frequently serves the purpose of concealing our thoughts, as Thomas Hobbes used to say about language in general, and unless a diagnostic label or technical term is actually required it should not be used. And if required it should be used after the case is worked out and analyzed, not instead of or before.

This case of Fish shows beyond any reasonable doubt that we deal here with a psychological condition which has a developmental history of growth and of structure—like a cancer, that may begin with an insignificant nodule, grow into a tumor, and spread and invade all the body organs until it kills the human organism.

This case of Fish demonstrates amply the vicissitudes of human aggression, its growth, its spread, its invasion of the total personality so that ultimately the personality dies (disintegrates) before the body does. The will power, the humanness of man is pervaded with the cancerous growth of mental disease, and what is left is a lot of primitive, savage drives wrapped in the thin paper of piety and clothed in a pale semblance of thinking. What is offered to the outside world is something that is no longer man, no longer will, no longer integrated comprehension, but merely here and there a flicker of a soul encased somewhere in a frame of self-propelled, cruel nothingness.

The mystery that is crime and hate, that baffling contradiction within one and the same person who is himself at once Christ and cannibal, and within whom sacrilege and worship live side by side without any sense of moral, logical, or practical contradiction—all these things cannot be understood, still less can such tragedies be prevented, unless we understand that a detailed developmental history of the personality in question is required. A superficial conclusion that there is nothing homicidal or suicidal, nothing criminal, etc., is easy, of course. Such conclusions do not do honor to those who make them; however, it is not only the psychiatrist who is guilty, but the system of superficial, bureaucratic disposition of a case in order to get on to the next one. Our whole system of pre-trial medical examination, the lack of funds, the overcrowded and understaffed state of the institutions required—all these together combine to make the problem almost sordid. There is as much justification for a psychiatrist to overlook the true personality that was Fish as there is for the committing judge to have the power to pass on the sanity of a patient.

I think in this connection of a woman, psychotic, who was brought from the ward of a mental hospital to be certified by a judge for commitment. A psychiatrist pointed out that the nature of the woman's illness was such that if not committed, if permitted to leave the hospital, she might very well kill her husband. The psychiatrist emphasized that this was in the nature of her psychotic trend regardless of her appearance. The judge in question had a talk with the woman *in camera* and concluded that he would deny the application for commitment because the woman appeared quite reasonable and she had promised to behave. She was let free. She was returned to the hospital less than two days later, this time not as a committed patient but to the prison ward as a criminal who had killed her husband.

The ways of human aggression are many, mysterious, not always predictable, but usually undetectable without careful, detailed psychiatric study which only the well-trained and experienced psychiatrist is capable of making or causing to have made under his guidance. Such study is a harsh, arduous, and at times frightening job, and cannot be performed by means of categorical definitions.

We could multiply the number of illustrative cases; there is, unfortunately, no dearth of cases of this sort. Unfortunately again, most of them are executed or otherwise put beyond the reach of psychiatric research. Something in our society seems not so much to neglect these studies as to oppose them. The law somehow, once it has got hold of the doer, wants to keep him out of sight. It wants to know very little more about him than the bare facts.

This is characteristic not only of our age. Thus we find

in our booklet by Sampson the following report of Catharine Ziegler, who was tried at Vienna for the murder of her bastard child. "She confessed the act, and said she could not possibly help it; she was forced to do it; she could not anyhow resist the desire she felt to commit the murder. The frankness of this her confession, connected with favourable circumstances, her good character, etc., induced the tribunal to pass a merciful sentence; and, on the ground of insanity (which she did not herself plead), she was acquitted, and at length let out of prison. But she told the court that, if they let her escape, they would be responsible for the next murder she committed, for that if she ever had a child again she should certainly kill it. And so in fact she did. About ten months after her release from prison, she was delivered of a child, which she soon murdered. Brought again to her trial, she repeated her old story; and added, that she became pregnant merely for the sake of having a child to kill. It does not appear whether she was brought before the same judges as before; most likely not; she was *executed* for this second murder." [5]

The clinically experienced psychiatrist long before Freud, like Georget, for instance, knew that women sometimes have infanticidal drives with the rest of their personality endowment seemingly remaining intact.

How contagious murderous aggression is, that is to say, how sensitized we are to it and therefore responsive to it, we may find from an extremely telling example cited by Gall, of a man who after witnessing an execution was seized with a desire to kill. If we recall the intimate relationships between murder and suicide in our psychic economy, we may understand a little better the pickpockets who plied

[5] Sampson, *op. cit.*, pp. 44-45.

their trade while within sight of the strangled criminal swinging from the gallows. After all, they had vicariously participated in the act of execution and also, therefore, had vicariously paid for their past crimes. This automatically brought them into a state of combined vicarious expiation and challenge against those righteous possessors of full pockets which they proceeded to pick with a complete sense of doing what they wanted to do, no matter what. This was their revenge for their own vicarious execution.

Aggression cannot be tempered without true psychological knowledge, and criminal and pathological forces cannot be stamped out with counter-aggression. It just does not work that way. For counter-aggression alone leaves a sense of futility in those who are responsible for the ultimate administration of justice. What can be more futile than to assume an attitude of hollow formalism in the face of a complex human problem?

Nothing can be more typical of what I have in mind than the testimony of those whose job it was to see that Fish was not insane before he went to the electric chair, or rather, that he was sane going to it.

It was established that Fish had auditory hallucinations, and also visual ones. The voices said something about Samson and Delilah, and he saw the face of Christ.

The prison psychiatrist stated simply: "No, he is not insane, just bad sex habits." The chaplain stated: "He tells me about the crime as though he were talking about something that might happen next day. He said he was sorry the little girl reminded him to take the instruments of torture he used; otherwise, she might have been alive today. He appears to have no conception of penitence."

Thus, during the final hours of his sordid life, the psychotic Fish was adjudged sane and justice ran its course.

The most flagrant psychological fact in the vicissitudes of aggression is the flattening and dulling of the emotional tone of the individual. He may speak as if he understands "the nature and consequences of his act," but if he does not feel it all adequately he is like a man who is awake, normal, rational—but totally anesthetic. Such a person is not a whole person. The considerable diminution or absence of emotion, of "affect" as we say, is probably the most virulent phenomenon leading to the paralysis of moral judgment and of will. Our laws have no provision for taking into account this extremely important psychological phenomenon, yet it has been observed and recognized for a long time. Perhaps this is what Pritchard sensed intuitively when he formulated his concept of "moral insanity" in 1834, a concept which Isaac Ray particularly cherished.

The dulling of emotions, the failure to feel has nothing to do with morality or immorality. It is both a cause and a result of many severe psychopathological reactions, and I am certain that it plays a major role in the development of all sorts of criminal personalities and their crimes. If the emotions are flattened and dull, we may understand pain in the manner that a blind man might possibly "understand" color—he would perceive it as something foreign to him. Under the circumstances, the aggressive drives would break through, since the barrier of feeling fails to arrest the action; the will cannot step in, as it were, and assert its control. The will can act only if that which is reason and that which is feeling are integrated. If they split off from one another even partially, the door to aggression opens to the extent of the diminution of affect. That which has become known in present-day psychoanalytic psychology as the ego—the very substance of the human personality—cannot function either in the direction of conscience or in the direction of virtue, unless it is fully integrated with adequate feeling tones—which seem to be more an essential ingredient of that which makes man "man" than mere intelligence and cold reason.

5.

SOME SOURCES OF THE DRIVE TO PUNISH

THE PROBLEM of how to evaluate a criminal's state of mind is not only complex but also very old. It is as puzzling as it is astonishing to what extent the confusion of legal and medical minds on this matter is almost a tradition rather than a condition which both jurist and doctor seem to try to combat.

I do not mean to say that both jurist and doctor traditionally connive to keep the perennial confusion untouched by light of science or charity. On the contrary, since the third decade of the sixteenth century, when Cornelius Agrippa stood up in open court and at the risk of his position and even his personal life tried to save an old village woman from the accusation that she was a witch, insisting that she was "melancholy" ("insane" in our modern language)—from that time on to date there has been an unsolved struggle in the hearts and the minds of the jurist and the doctor: to convict or not to convict. This struggle, I believe, does not spring from the aspiration to be just and serve the ideal of justice; it is actually a psychological struggle, that is to say, an intrapsychic struggle of other forces within those who deal with the accused. For no one, no matter how well convinced that the guilty ought to be punished, dares to say the word "guilty" without somehow wanting to share the responsibility with someone else.

Some time ago, in a classroom of mine, a student raised

[69]

the question as to what ought to be done with a man like Carl Hall, the confessed murderer of Bobby Greenlease. The student had very strong feelings about the matter. She wanted Carl Hall destroyed, electrocuted. There was so much conviction and intensity in her voice that I asked her whether she would accept the role of Carl Hall's executioner. She demurred. It is easier to condemn than to execute; it is easier to say "guilty" than to sentence. This it seems to me is the chief psychological reason why the recent report of the Royal Commission would shift more responsibility onto the jury and thus relieve the judge from being forced to pronounce a mandatory sentence of death. Justice, in the sense of being just, is frequently done a disservice as a result of this inner struggle which each and every participant in a criminal trial experiences whether he knows it or not.

Let us not be deceived by the progress of psychological science, or by our alleged progress in general. The struggle of one man against another man who violates his property or life is very old, very intense, elemental; from the psychological point of view it is the same today as it was centuries ago.

Among the many interesting cases cited by Isaac Ray, the one of Henriette Cornier is typical and very instructive:

"Henriette Cornier, a female servant aged twenty-seven years, was of a mild and lively disposition, full of gaiety, and remarkably fond of children. In the month of June, 1825, a singular change was observed in her character; she became silent, melancholy, absorbed in reverie, and finally sank into a kind of stupor. She was dismissed from her place, but her friends could obtain from her no account of the causes of her mental dejection. In the month of September she made an attempt to commit suicide, but was prevented. In the following October she entered into the service of dame Fournier, but there she still presented the melancholic and desponding disposition. Dame Fournier observed her peculiar dejection and endeavored in vain to ascertain its cause; the girl would talk only of her misfortunes in losing her parents at an early age; and of the bad treatment she received from her guardian. On the 4th of November, her conduct not having been previously different from what it usually was, she suddenly conceived and immediately executed the act for which she was committed.

"About noon her mistress went out to walk, having told Cornier to prepare dinner at the usual hour, and to go to a neighboring shop kept by dame Belon, to buy some cheese. She had frequently gone to this shop and had always manifested great fondness for Belon's little girl, a beautiful child, nineteen months old. On this day she displayed her usual fondness for it, and persuaded its mother, who at first was rather unwilling, to let her take it out for a walk. Cornier then hastened back to her mistress's house with the child. [She quickly killed the child.] . . . She subsequently declared that while executing this horrid deed, she felt no particular emotion—neither of pleasure, nor of pain. . . .

"She made no attempt to escape, nor to deny the crime; she confessed all the circumstances, even her premeditated design and the perfidy of her caresses, which had persuaded the unhappy mother to entrust her with the child. It was found impossible to excite in her the slightest emotion of remorse or grief; to all that was said, she replied with indifference, 'I intended to kill the child.' When closely and earnestly interrogated, as to her motives for committing this dreadful act, she replied that she had no particular reason for it; that the idea had taken possession of her mind, and that she was destined to do it. When asked why she threw the head into the street, she answered that it was for the purpose of attracting public attention, so that people might come up to her chamber and see that she alone was guilty. The nature of her extraordinary replies, the want of motives for such an atrocious deed, the absence of every kind of emotion, and the state of stupor in which she remained, fixed the attention of the medical men who were called in, and impressed them with the belief that she was mad. On the examination before the magistrate she confirmed the above statements respecting her mental condition, adding, among other things, that she had been unhappily married seven years before; that she attempted to drown herself 'because she was ennuied at changing her place of service so often'; that she knew her crime deserved death and she desired it.

"She was tried for the first time, on the 27th of February, 1826. She then appeared to be in a state of great nervous irritation; her limbs trembled; her eyes were fixed; and her understanding was dull and stupid. A few days previously, the court, at the request of her counsel, appointed a medical commission consisting of Adelon, Esquirol, and Leveillé, to examine the accused and all the documents of the case, and report on her 'actual moral state.' Accordingly they reported that they were unable to detect any sign or proof of mental derangement; but added that it is extremely difficult in some cases, to establish the existence of insanity, it requiring a long intimacy with the individual and numerous opportunities of watching him under every variety of circumstance, none of which they had possessed in this case.

In fine, they reported that though they could not adduce any positive proof of her insanity, yet they were equally unable to pronounce her sane.

"This report not being satisfactory, the trial was postponed to another session, and the prisoner was sent to the Salpétrière to be observed by the above-named physicians. After recapitulating their observations which were continued three months, they came to the following conclusions: 'first, that during the whole time Cornier was under examination, from the 25th of February to the 3rd of June, they had observed in regard to her moral state great mental dejection, extreme dullness of mind, and profound chagrin; secondly, that the actual situation of Cornier sufficiently explains her moral state, and thus does not of itself indicate mental alienation either general or partial.' They also added that it was due to the cause of justice and to their own conscience, to declare that their judgment of her actual moral condition could not be considered final, if it were proved, as stated in the *acte d'accusation*, that long before the 4th of November, the character and habits had changed; that she had become sad, gloomy, silent and restless; for then that which might be attributed to her present situation, could be only the continuation of a melancholic state that had existed for a year.

"Cornier was again brought to trial on the 24th of June, and the jury returned a verdict of guilty of 'committing homicide voluntarily but not with premeditation'; and accordingly she was sentenced to hard labor for life." [1]

Isaac Ray reminds us that Georget, the youngest yet the most brilliant medico-legal mind of the time, censured this

[1] Ray, *op. cit.*, pp. 219-23.

verdict saying: ". . . if the accused was mad she ought to have been acquitted; and if not mad she acted from pre-meditation, and should have suffered the punishment of death." [2]

Yet the obvious straddling on the part of the jury and the court is not due to any lack of reasoning power on the part of those concerned. It is due primarily to the fact that a decision in a given criminal case is pre-eminently an emotional decision. Whether you call it public opinion, the conscience of the jury, the skill or wisdom of the defending or the prosecuting attorneys, we are dealing with that which we have learned to recognize in modern psychology as deeply seated affects, deep-seated emotional currents which move men to act more often than their realistic reason and will would let them, and in directions which are at times contrary to the very core of rational behavior.

I am reminded in this connection of an episode which occurred in open court within the hearing of everyone, and the astonishing thing about it was that no one appeared surprised. The prosecutor was hammering at an expert witness, a psychiatrist. The witness expressed the opinion that the defendant was a good Catholic. "How do you know that the defendant is a good Catholic?" shouted the prosecutor, himself a Catholic. The witness gave his reasons and added that on the basis of these reasons he, the witness, felt that he would follow in the footsteps of St. Paul and in the spirit of charity consider that the defendant's acts of devotion and worship were signs of her being a good Catholic. The retort was quite telling: "I too believe in St. Paul and charity, but in the right place." The witness reminded the

2 *Ibid.*, p. 223.

prosecutor that St. Paul did not happen to ration charity. The prosecutor did not reply.

This rationing of charity is merely a manifestation of the punitive attitude which we feel inwardly toward a criminal, even if we are not called upon to play the role of official prosecutor. We struggle against whatever impulse of charity we might experience. It is not a question of following the dictum: "He who is without sin should be the first to throw a stone at her." Rather, it is a desire: Let us stone her! But the voice of conscience or charity rebels against this impulse, and a silly compromise is reached: let us not stone her, but let us throw at her a few social stones, or many stones, or just one or two as the case happens to be.

As you see, I am trying to lay emphasis on the aggressive, punitive impulses of the agencies of justice rather than on the purely metaphysical philosophy of just punishment. In this respect we are confronted with the same psychological problem we dealt with when we considered the criminal act—namely, the problem of aggression. The court, the prosecutor, the jury, insofar as they are punitive agents, are all motivated by their aggressive reactions toward the criminal. The agencies of justice might therefore be called agencies of counter-aggression against the aggressor called a criminal.

Those who are inclined to see in this view merely an oversimplification, with too much emphasis on purely psychological considerations, would do well to consider how the same mode of thinking, the same manner and method might lead to different conclusions. Thus Duns Scotus, the subtle doctor of the late thirteenth century, would consider all crime as coming from madness, and since crime must be punished, no madman ought to be exempt from punishment if he commits a crime. On the other hand, St. Thomas, the older contemporary of Scotus, would exempt the same criminals from punishment on the same grounds, that they happen to be madmen.[3]

On the surface, the above is merely an example of scholastic subtleties. But in actuality it illustrates a fundamental attitude which has more than a note of contemporary contentions. For this is an example of what people mistakenly call *temperamental* difference, which is another way of saying differences in emotional attitudes. Those emotional attitudes are very often unconscious yet potent, and they determine, as it were, who shall be and stay a prosecutor and who shall be and stay a defense attorney.

The conclusion therefore imposes itself upon us that the psychological, affective motivations in favor of punishment are the very same as the ones which lead man to commit a transgression of the law. It might appear a bit difficult and even distasteful to the uninitiated to accept this formulation. It does, and instead we frequently hear that the criminal law and its procedural adjuncts are true defenders of society.

You will recall what I have said about the tendency to assert that criminal behavior is primarily antisocial behavior. To some extent, and only from a certain point of view, it is; but from the psychological point of view it is an act of aggression on the part of a person who is as a rule rather egocentric, with extremely attenuated social feelings. His transgressions look antisocial, but in actuality they are but self-centered acts of aggression without any regard for society at all. Many contemporary writers on the subject of delinquency have recognized this psychological fact and

[3] *Ibid.*, p. 52.

have therefore tried to introduce new terms instead of the term "antisocial." Redl speaks of "pseudo-social" behavior and, earlier, Aichhorn spoke of "dissocial" behavior.

Our views of the criminal law as protector and defender of society will (at least from the psychological point of view) also have to be revised. After all, there is no criminal law which would permit the arrest and punishment of anyone who merely planned to commit a crime and revealed to no one his plans. The law must wait till the crime is committed before it steps in. If the crime is an antisocial act, one can hardly call the penal laws defenders of society, since they wait till the antisocial act is first committed and thus injury to society has been done. We must bear in mind also that punishment, despite the traditional belief to the contrary, has apparently no deterrent effects on crime. Since punishment does not precede but follows the antisocial act and, in addition, does not seem to exercise any deterrent effect on crime, it would be a gross error indeed to consider the traditional penal system as a system of social defense.

It is perhaps more in the American tradition than any other, particularly since William A. White's studies in criminology were made, to view the aggressive aspects of our penal system as being the most characteristic ones. William A. White did not hesitate to say that the criminal law is more revengeful than rational and just, and that it represents more hostility against the criminal than concern about the safety of the body social.

We ought not to be shocked at this particular appraisal of our penological system. For, essentially, the history of the development of our punitive law represents an excellent illustration of the psychological conflict between aggression

and pity, between hatred and charity, between revengeful-
ness and forgiveness.

Take as an instance the older method of trial and punishment. We need not go into all the gruesome and loathsome
details. The fact remains that in the course of the last two
or three centuries the punishment of criminals has become
humanized, as the saying goes. The law and our society
as a whole are proud of this humanization.

Yet, if it is true that the punishment of the criminal must
have a deterrent effect, then the abolition of the drawing
and quartering of criminals was both a logical and penological mistake. Why make punishment milder and thus
diminish the deterrent effect of punishment? There was a
time when people stood up in the House of Commons and
pleaded not to abolish capital punishment for the theft of
five shillings, for fear that no house would be safe with
hosts of five-shilling thieves descending upon and intruding
into the homes of England.

There is no logical reason why our punishment has become more humane, but there is a good emotional, psychological reason. In the course of the past three or even four
centuries, the general evolution of our society, European
and American, has led to a greater socialization of our individual interests and thus to a greater appreciation of what
is usually called individual freedom. This evolution has led
inevitably to an enhanced capacity on each individual's
part for identification with another individual. All human
beings are equal, not because they are really equal but
because we are able to put ourselves in the place of so
many others, and we thus feel equal with so many others.

It is this psychological equality that produces a paradoxical attitude toward the criminal. We, so-called normal peo-

ple, know without knowing it, feel without being aware of it, the degree to which we are inwardly tempted in all directions of aggression and depravity. As Freud put it so tartly, the law does not forbid that which man is not prone to do. Therefore, "Thou shalt not kill" or "Thou shalt not covet thy neighbor's wife" are not merely abstract dicta, general, spontaneously invented prohibitions against the deeds of some few unknown and as yet undiscovered evil men. On the contrary, these are commandments issued for the guidance of the average man with average propensities. Cain was not a unique, perverted deviation of manhood, and Abraham was not a unique, evil father who in order to flatter the Lord was ready to butcher his son. In other words, the average man is the carrier of the very impulses which are called criminal when they are acted out.

This consideration should not throw us into a state of gloom and make us look upon man with definitive pessimism. Between the Platonic essential pessimism as to the nature of man and the Aristotelian optimism, we may well assume the attitude of psychological realism which remained unknown to both Plato and Aristotle. This psychological realism is not a static nor a fatalistic view. It is merely an empirical evaluation of man in action; it is a point of view which takes into consideration the unconscious of man and the totality of his instinctual life.

Armed with this knowledge and point of view, we can understand better the paradoxical attitude toward the criminal on the part of modern man. On the one hand we identify ourselves with the criminal's own impulses, and consequently we are tempted to give vent to those impulses within us which are usually inhibited. This state of temptation produces anxiety unless it is lived out in some innocent way such as the reading of detective stories and murder mysteries. Our anxiety can be quieted down only in one of two ways: in our sudden, unconscious denial of any similarity with the criminal, we can hurl ourselves upon him with all the power of our aggressive, punitive, destructive hostility; or, we can assume the criminal to be a mentally sick man and can then assume a more tolerant, more charitable attitude toward the doer if not the deed.

In those days when ascetic ideals were particularly widespread and at the same time threatened by the Reformation, the cruelty and atrocious refinement of torture took precedence over charity for sinners. This seemed to be the only way in which a passing ascetic world was able to defend itself against a new loosening of the principles of life and morals. It is both frightening and instructive to observe how whenever in the history of mankind there is an increase of self-centered psychology, of the psychology of self-righteousness of the powers that be, there is an increase of cruelty in relation to transgressions of the law and an increase in the refinement of human torture. Our own generation has seen examples of it in many a spot in our changing world. On the other hand, the socialization of our minds, the increase in the sense of interdependence of our lives, produces a tendency to identify ourselves with the transgressors, to "humanize" our mode of punishment, and thus to work against the very principle which penal law has officially adopted for ages: the deterrent effect of punishment.

The law is a slow-moving body of human reactions articulated into formulas and ritualized in procedure. Therefore, the criminal law cannot yet reflect the influence of Freudian psychology. It cannot recognize the unconscious, for criminal law is based on a set of psycho-sociological reactions which are so deeply rooted in the psychological history of mankind that by its very nature it must stand closer to the older *lex talionis,* trial by ordeal and the spirit of revenge. After all, hardly three hundred years have passed since Lord Hale, while considering all criminals madmen (in the manner of Duns Scotus), still wished to destroy all criminals. The psychological undercurrents of present-day penal codes are but a short distance removed from the older spirit of revenge.

This is the reason why two contemporary writers, a doctor and a lawyer, felt justified in saying in their recent book [4] that a present-day criminal trial is not a scientific investigation after truth but an adversary proceeding; in other words, it is a fight between adversaries each of whom is actuated only by the personal desire to win. "Adversary" in this case is but a euphemism for "enemy." The most typical characteristic of the struggle between enemies is that they are not intent on saving anybody (not even the defendant, I am tempted to say) but only on winning their own battle, on annihilating their adversary.

Without going into any detail as to procedure in a criminal trial, it is easy to see that both the defense and the prosecution are out to win. No matter how benevolent and well-meaning the men who happen to represent the defense and the prosecution may be, it is psychologically impossible under the present system of law and procedure for them to rid themselves of that self-centered, purely narcissistic need to win. Consequently, the defendant all too often becomes merely a catalytic agent, a stimulant in the adversary proceeding. The prosecutor may have a chance to mobilize his ability to hate, which he may turn onto the defendant;

[4] Guttmacher and Weihofen, *op. cit.*

the defense attorney may turn his hate on the prosecution, but he can hardly turn his love and charity toward the defendant, for he is too busy fighting. In other words, the defendant as a person, as a human being, all too often stands a perfect chance of being forgotten, since he is but a tool in the duel between two narcissisms: defense and prosecution.

I cannot repeat too often and too emphatically that I am not passing any judgment on the validity of our criminal procedure or the justice or injustice of it. I cannot and would not do this for the simple reason that our system of criminal law is a product of many centuries of human relations which cannot be changed at the whim of even a philanthropically-minded psychopathologist. This consideration, however, should not deter us from making an attempt to understand the psychological factors which are brought into play in the administration of our present-day criminal justice.

A word about the judge and jury. It is before them as the microcosm of public opinion that the adversary proceeding is displayed. The judge, particularly when there is a jury, plays the conservative role; he is the law pure and simple. As a human being he may betray his weaknesses and here and there reveal a bias, but on the whole, insofar as he is the official representative of the tradition of the law and insofar as the law is punitive, the judge is of necessity forced into the difficult psychological position of never forgetting that the law is punitive. This, I say, is the psychological position in the majority of cases; that is why public opinion speaks more often of hanging judges and forgets those judges who direct the jury to return a verdict of not guilty or dismiss a case entirely.

In other words, the substance of the punitive law as the law of vengeance upon the accused is not much changed as a rule by the role assigned to the judge.

The jury represents a different and difficult problem. In cases in which a death sentence is a possibility, the law from the very outset puts the accused at a disadvantage and thus increases its revengeful spirit. For any jurymen who have reservations against capital punishment are automatically excluded from the jury box. Those who are left present in advance a group of people who are committed not to hesitate to condemn a man to death if they think him guilty—and who knows what motivations might be set into play in the minds and the heads of a jury when they deal with a particularly tough case of brutal murder. Albert Fish was thus convicted and sentenced to death. So was the young man Volkmann, aged nineteen, who was a typical schizophrenic, probably of the catatonic type. So was Fiorenza, who was executed at the age of twenty-one, than whom there was no more typical schizophrenic; seven years before he committed the murder he was in a reformatory, and even then he was considered by the psychiatrist in charge as dangerous and apt to commit murder. (The state had its authoritative hand firmly on Fiorenza seven years before he killed Mrs. Titterton, and the true tragedy of our modern society is best illustrated by this case: The state steps in only after the fact, not before, even if it has a chance. The two most important functions of the penal system which modern criminology demands, preventive and restorative, seem as yet far from being efficiently exercised by the state. We need not go into the question why this is so. This is a topic for a separate discussion outside the confines set for the present one.)

One added word about the jury system. It is too bad, of course, that such scientific questions as the presence or absence of mental illness are frequently left to the jury to answer. The jury finds itself saddled with this problem under certain circumstances even in the State of New Hampshire, where "insanity" is considered a question of fact and is supposed to be settled by the psychiatrists of the state.

Yet from the psychological point of view a court without a jury would be left (I have in mind criminal trials only) without that vague, intuitive apparatus which alone is apt to act without the self-centered personalism of other agencies of the court trial. If we bear in mind that 80 per cent [5] of all delinquents and criminals are characterologically similar to the average population, the jury represents the only body through which could be refracted all the possibilities of guilt, forgiveness, and a corresponding diminution of that spirit of revenge which represents all the criminal laws of all known penal systems. I would not want to insist that the jury is the only corrective. And I doubt whether it is a sure corrective. But as I have said, taking into consideration the play of particular psychological forces which are so active in a criminal trial, the jury represents the factor least afflicted with that narcissistic spirit which is characteristic of the adversary proceeding under consideration.

There is for the moment nothing to suggest but to take our penal system and its procedural aspects as given; for the substance of these seems to be deeply entrenched in the instinctual psychology of our human community and

[5] Daniel Lagache, *"Psycho-Criminogenèse."* From the 10th General Report: 2me Congrès International de Criminologie, Paris, September 10-19, 1950.

even at the risk of appearing too pessimistic, one is loath to suggest any specific reform. Reforms in this particular field are extremely slow and quite rare. And such reforms are more concerned with the adjective than with the substantive aspects of the problem.

We may recall in this connection and with considerable profit that the most recent task of the Royal Commission was definitely circumscribed in that, while charged with the job of dealing with capital punishment, it was specifically instructed not to consider the abolition of this punishment. Let us also recall the recent temporary abolition of capital punishment in England, during a period of less than five years, and the singular anxiety of the community lest a definitive step toward abolition would be taken. Let us also recall that in the course of the last few years there was strong agitation in Switzerland in favor of the re-establishment of capital punishment for burglaries. Since the war the number of burglaries showed an alarming increase in Switzerland. As you see, the solution suggested by the most authoritative criminologists of the country was again a punitive one: more punishment, that is to say, more nondeterring deterrents.

It does seem obvious that scientific progress in criminology has been made in the field of detection of crime, and in the organization of policing activities. But it does seem also that we are still far from a truly scientific approach to the problem of dealing with the criminal. We are quite a distance from this approach, because the impulse to take revenge, the talion principle regardless of what its manifestation in the law may be, is still the preponderant principle of our penal system.

The trouble in the whole matter is primarily this: Criminal law, whatever its apparent accouterments of modern dress, still seems to look upon mankind as roughly divided into two groups: good people and bad people, men of good will (or of no ill will) and men of ill will. The degree of ill will is usually measured by the degree of damage done by the accused to property and to life—a gross way of measuring to be sure, but a characteristic one. Such a way of measuring takes into consideration only the manifestation of the ill will of the accused, not even the nature of the ill will itself. In other words, a certain aspect of the function of the personality seems to be separated, and quite artificially, from the rest and then examined with the cold eye of the punitive principle.

On the other hand, modern psychology and our increasing social consciousness have opened vistas on the human personality heretofore unsuspected and introduced socio-ethical perspectives heretofore unenvisaged. As a result, those who study young delinquents and older criminals are literally unable to approach such study with the artificiality which was ours through the ages. We can no longer take one single aspect of the human personality and study it as if it were a separate thing, even if it be the ill will of a bad man. We must study the human being in his totality, and the personality of the criminal is no more divisible than that of an honest man.

That is why such studies as Bowlby's,[6] of forty-four thieves as compared with forty-four non-thieves, demonstrate conclusively what depths we must reach to understand how a

[6] J. Bowlby, "Forty-four Juvenile Thieves: Their Character and Home Life," *International Journal of Psycho-Analysis*, Vol. 25, 1944.

person embarks on a criminal career or becomes subject to impulsive criminal acts. The more we study these problems, the more obvious it becomes that the older concepts of quick justice have long outlived their usefulness, that is, unless we wish to preserve the spirit of revenge in our justice, instead of the spirit of rehabilitation of the man who erred—no matter how brutal and bloody his error.

This objection to quick justice was raised authoritatively even one hundred and fifteen years ago by Isaac Ray, who said, commenting on the manner in which the case of Henriette Cornier was handled: "What a contrast does this calm and deliberate inquiry present to the indecent haste with which the legal proceedings were precipitated against Bellingham, who committed his offence, was indicted, tried and hung, all within a space of eight days." [7] This manner of bringing the criminal to justice quickly is but a reflection of the general tendency of the courts and of society to get rid of the evildoer as quickly as possible in order to forget the deed itself. Throughout the ages stress has been laid primarily on the deed itself. As to who committed it—all the courts apparently needed was the positive identification of the accused as the doer.

To be sure, today we have reports of probation officers, and in certain cases even psychiatric reports. But the most conscientious probation officer is not an experienced, skilled psychologist, and he cannot offer a sufficiently detailed study of the accused. On the other hand, if and when a psychiatric report is at hand, how jealously some district attorneys keep these reports from the counsel for the defense until the day of the trial—as if to know and understand the accused is of

[7] Ray, *op. cit.*, p. 62.

no or at any rate secondary importance, but to secure a conviction is a goal of first and penultimate importance.

This is the spirit of an adversary proceeding, but it perpetuates the tradition of revenge, of aggression on the part of criminal law. It does not help to save man, and still less to save society.

6.

SOME FURTHER ASPECTS OF
PUNISHMENT

EVEN at the risk of appearing repetitious and senten-
tious, I must remind the reader that these pages
deal primarily with the psychology of the criminal
act and with that system of justice which responds to this
act with formal, legal punishment. I will not enter here
into any discussion as to what is right and what is wrong
from the purely moral point of view, or as to what is legal
or illegal.

Nor do I plan any excursion into the philosophy of punitive law. I am aware, of course, that the study of the psychology of anything that is human at once brings us into
contact with ethics, theology, philosophy, and, in this case,
the philosophy of law in particular. Therefore, any contact
with the above-mentioned disciplines which I may have be-
trayed thus far is purely coincidental and accidental, and
the reader may, and ought to disregard it as much as possible by focusing his attention only on the psychological
aspects of the various problems which I have presented.

My plea may appear rather singular, particularly at this
point when I stand committed by my own statements to a
certain critical orientation for whose support I seem to in-
voke some of the insights which modern psychology offers
us. Yet my plea at this particular moment is neither singular
nor presented too late. It is presented here and now because,
as we reviewed the revengeful and almost sterile features of

the punitive aspects of the law, we must have become aware of a serious and unsolved, agelong conflict within ourselves and within the civilized society to which we belong and of which we have become only rather cautiously proud in recent years. Perhaps this conflict can best be illustrated by a telling fact which was a part of Warden Lawes's experiences in Sing Sing Prison.

Whether it is the requirement of the law or of tradition, I do not know, but it is customary that an invitation to attend the execution of a criminal is usually sent to the prosecuting attorney and to the sentencing judge of any given case. This seems a rather reasonable custom. After all, to the prosecutor who succeeded in convincing the jury that the supreme penalty must be paid, and to the judge who officiated in pronouncing the ultimate demands of the law, to them more than to anyone else ought to belong the distinction of being witnesses that final justice is done. At first glance, particularly if we recall the ardor of some prosecutors and the sternness of some judges, it would seem that these officials would be glad (every now and then, at least) to come and behold the ultimate legal result of some unpardonable, heinous crime. Yet Warden Lawes relates that he faithfully sent out an invitation to the prosecutors and judges concerned with every one of the 114 executions which were carried out during his tenure of office, and not once did a prosecutor or judge come to witness the final act of the law.

I am sure that we experience a sense of sympathetic understanding and that we do not blame the jurists concerned for this their steadfast absenteeism. We do not blame them for apparently feeling that they had performed their duty before the law and on the bench, and that that was enough. Perhaps it was. If it was, why was it?

The answer is really simple: Those who condemn and sentence feel somewhere within themselves rather burdened. That which they have done, they claim, and not without right, is an unpleasant duty which their office requires them to perform. The striking thing about this psychological situation is the contrast between the intensity of conviction displayed by the jurist, and even his harsh vituperation *before* the accused is adjudged guilty and sentenced, and the almost lamblike humility of the same jurist when an opportunity is offered him to see with his own eyes the factual, palpable results of that which he demanded in the name of the law and with a rightful sense of conscience and public service. The modern psychological terminology would describe this humility after the conviction and sentence, this avoidance of following up the course of events, this deliberate lack of curiosity, as a form of turning away from certain of the ultimate consequences of the jurist's own efforts.

All this is very human. It is very human to be ambivalent, which means not only to be of two minds as the saying goes, but to be of two hearts, so to speak, about the things one does and accomplishes. In other words, the prosecutor and judge as representatives of the law are the carriers of one of the oldest and most solemn and painful traditions of mankind—the tradition of the law, the tradition of formalized and sanctified power of one man over another, of the power of one man to judge the other and the power of one man to lay hands on the other with the full weight of that which is both solemn and cruel, determined yet slowly deliberative—that which is covered by the justifiably hallowed name of law and justice. Yet who would be so bold and so unreasonable as to deny that he who is the true representative of law and justice, like the priest who is the man of God, is also man—small in his very greatness, weak in his very power, fearful in his very courage, and capable (almost inevitably so) of feeling guilty in the very midst of his rightfully and righteously fulfilling the demands of the law.

It would be silly therefore to picture every prosecuting attorney as merely a sadist at heart, and every "hanging" judge as one who lives on human suffering. No, they are men, simple men within themselves, simply driven into action by a number of their natural propensities. I do not mean to say they are automatons, purely mechanistic products of a deterministic world. They are free men with free consciences and free human wills—all enmeshed in the tangle of contradictory human relations and unconscious, potent trends.

No human act can be properly understood either by the scientist or the moral teacher without taking into consideration these potent, unconscious reactions with which our human self, our ego as it is technically called, defends itself against many a painful, conflictive situation. These defenses are also unconscious, and most of them are or have become automatic. The pathologist as well as the undertaker, each in his own way, must find a psychological (unconscious) method of defending himself against the constant reminder of the daily monotony of death and its threat of nothingness. Well, the pathologist as well as the undertaker "knows" certainly better than the anxious neurotic person how not to be aware of, how to *deny* death. This is the fascinating paradox of man's existence: he may deal with death daily, he may professionally and verbally assert its existence and practically utilize it to derive scientific or economic benefit from it, yet emotionally, psychologically he may remain cheerful, happy, full of verve and inspiration, serve life fully as a father, a citizen, or a servant of God.

This psychological denial is what makes us what we are: human. The more we are able to integrate our anxieties with our psychological defenses and live with them together as if they were unified into one living drive, the healthier and more alive we are. The more torn we are by this our ambivalence, or our many ambivalences, the more tormented we are both consciously and unconsciously, and the unhealthier we are psychologically.

We may recall the gravedigger in *Hamlet*. The gravedigger cracked a joke as soon as he picked up the skull, and he thought of life. To him the skull was just a thing. Of course he knew whose skull it was, or he could know; of course he could reflect on the problem of life and death in his own manner. But no matter—he was just a gravedigger, psychologically divorced from the skeletons that once were bodies. On the other hand, he who felt so guilty of murder actual and/or intended, Hamlet, was overwhelmed with emotions in which the consciousness of death was so much greater; hence Hamlet's soliloquy—an expression of pain, horror, fear, and regret.

Our social organization, particularly our system of justice, utilizes our human ambivalence and the inner conflicts which result from it, and utilizes them with extreme sensitiveness and discrimination—almost with scientific precision. The only reason why I would avoid calling it scientific is that it is all a product of historico-psychological evolution and not merely a deliberate and skillful distribution of labor between various unconscious psychological factors which Freud was fortunate enough to discover.

This brings us back to our prosecuting attorneys and sentencing judges who never come to witness an execution which they have been instrumental in bringing about. It is the second component of their ambivalence, their sense of guilt, that keeps them away from the concluding scene of the judicial drama. In this they are unwittingly representing the sense of guilt which hovers in the hearts and minds of all members of our civilized community. This sense of guilt is as integral an element of our psychology of legal justice as the sense of revenge of which I spoke earlier. We must remember, therefore, that this sense of guilt is both a result of the revengeful spirit of legal punishment and an indication that punishment pure and simple, no matter how correctly and legally meted out, does not fully satisfy our human conscience. And by the same token, punishment fails to carry out its avowed goal: deterrence, penitence, and rehabilitation.

It is perhaps timely to state here that I am fully aware of the main currents of philosophical and sociological and ethical thought dealing with law and punishment. And I do not believe it is really necessary to review these currents here. Those interested are referred to any authoritative treatise on the subject of philosophy and law, and they will find, throughout the great variety of schools of thought, the same groping through the same forest of motivations. From Thomas Aquinas to our contemporaries, through Locke and Rousseau, Joseph de Maistre and Jeremy Bentham, through James or John Stuart Mill and Lombroso to our own day, we hear that society has a right to punish, that people are afraid of punishment, and that delinquent

behavior is halted *ex timore poenae.* Some theologians deny
that punishment for crime is of divine sanction and origin,
and insist that it is in temporal power only that the right to
punish resides, that this right to punish is in pursuit of
certain purely sociological goals; in other words, they imply
that expiation is really not the goal of penal law, and that
divine vengeance is different from the vengeance of the law.
And it is the term "vengeance" that was used by the six-
teenth-, seventeenth-, and eighteenth-century writers on the
subject.

What is remarkable and most telling is that whatever the
school of thought and whatever the ethico-religious orientation of the thinkers and writers on the subject, the question as to what is achieved by punishment is answered
always in terms of general principles: fear of suffering, paying one's debt to society, reasserting the dignity and inviola-
bility of the social order, etc. In other words, there are more
stated goals which the penologists wish to achieve than
demonstrations of actual achievement.

There is a singular prevalence of assertions of unproven
sociological facts. It has not been proved that the systematic
burning of witches finally eradicated witchcraft on this
earth; I doubt whether it can be proved that crime is eliminated by punishment, or by punishment alone. I doubt
whether the world was saved from perdition at the hands
of universal witchcraft by the systematic burning of witches
and sorcerers, as I doubt that the world is saved from being
overwhelmed by lawlessness and crime because of the penal
system as it is practiced today, and as a matter of principle
has been practiced since time immemorial—long before
the advent of Christianity, and after it when the most
earnest theologians of the Church became preoccupied with

the problems of differentiating sin from legal transgression and religious sanctions from temporal ones.

By the thirteenth century the problems of penology had become sufficiently crystallized so that in the *Summa Theologica* we find most of what had been repeated through the previous centuries (and since) on the subject of the common good and the order which society must protect by punishment, including capital punishment; that the common good is superior in value to personal good; therefore that willful violation of the law is a crime against society and its demands. There seems to be little doubt that an orderly and well-regulated society is the lawgiver, and that that giver of the law has a right to exact its pound of flesh.

As you see, there is no real psychological evaluation in all this. (There is very little even in any of the sociological schools such as those of Gabriel Tarde or Emile Durkheim, the fathers of modern sociology, who, despite their leanings toward psychology, remained quite unpsychological and positivistic.) There is little if any consideration here of the psychology of the individual who without becoming a martyr to a cause is yet inspired by motivations other than the established order. It is not enough to proclaim that man is a social animal and that society is a natural phenomenon and therefore of divine origin. We know that people who are usually law-abiding, peaceful human beings under conditions of wars and revolutions suddenly find themselves fully at the mercy of their basest and most brutal instincts. This will occur in the atmosphere of a most punitive order as well as a most permissive one—as in various phases of revolutions and wars during the last thirty-five to forty years or so. Punishment pure and simple appears then to be a true manifestation of that revengeful power-seeking, that

instinct of domination which society may adopt as a form
of rationalized self-protection.

I may therefore repeat that without psychological insight
there can be no rational penological system, no true justice.
The belief that society serves the common and individual
good by a system of rigid punishment has never been fully
justified by history, and its persistence looks more and more
like superstition than a conviction based on fact. For one
thing must never be forgotten, one thing that Thomas
Aquinas saw clearly almost seven hundred years ago; while
accepting the more or less formal and traditional view on
punishment, he asserted that punishment, in order to prove
fully effective and therefore satisfactory and serve the purpose of rehabilitation, *must be accepted* by the one on
whom the punishment is meted out.[1] The center of attention is then the person of the transgressor, not the latter's
repentance before punishment, but his wish to accept the
suffering of punishment.

This acceptance of suffering in order to reform is psychologically and sociologically different from that desire to
suffer which we find in criminals who seek suffering and
use crime only as a vehicle for masochistic gratification.
To accept suffering as a result of crime means to accept it
emotionally, which in turn means to undergo a certain type
of reconstruction within one's self which produces a new
or renewed sense of being one with the social totality within
one's own self. This type of reconstruction requires first of
all time and considerable emotional reworking of the various aspects of one's self. This is true of the neurotic as well
as of the habitual thief, although the habitual thief may

---

[1] Thomas Aquinas, *Summa Theologica*, I, II, qu. 87, a. 6.

not suffer from any neurosis. However, both in the neurotic and the thief or murderer there must be a will in the direction of rehabilitation.

In cases of neurosis Freud called it the will to get well. Without that will, one could not get well—not easily at any rate. Most neurotics have this will to a greater or lesser extent, although at times it is necessary to work hard to awaken in a given neurotic the necessary will. How much more difficult a task is faced by the penologist and practical criminologist! For here the will to resocialization, or reintegration, or to reincorporation into one's self of certain standards so that they become one's own, this will must be awakened and not stifled by the act of punishment.

As a result of the development of modern psychology we are today perhaps at the threshold of a new change, a most important one in the history of mankind—a change of our views on the technique of application and practical utilization of punishment. It is true, of course, that our misconception of punishment, of its social and psychological and ethical value, is so old and so great that one might at times despair, but history knows of many radical changes in the field. St. Augustine considered a duel not only legitimate but a true manner of attaining justice. In a letter to Boniface he wrote: "During the combat, God waits, the heavens open, and He defends the person who is right." [2] In the sixth century Gregory of Tours still considered the duel an instrument serving to reveal the judgment of God. During the ninth century there appeared a strong opposition against dueling, but we had to wait almost seven hundred years till the Council of Trent condemned it and

[2] René Allendy, *La justice intérieure,* Paris, 1931, pp. 56 ff. [Translation is mine.]

prescribed excommunication of those engaged in dueling; approximately between the tenth and twelfth centuries dueling was still highly honored. The loser of a duel would then be considered guilty and sentenced to a punishment for his crime. As late as 1810, the French penal code says nothing about dueling, thus silently recognizing its inability to combat it. Nowadays, this method of justice seems to be almost entirely gone, except for its transformed inheritor in the courtroom, the duel between the defense and the prosecution. The origin of this latter duel does seem to have its psychological roots in the ancient form of justice by combat and revenge.

René Allendy, one of the earliest psychological writers who devoted a great deal of energy to the study of the problems of justice and punishment, made the following observation:

If we compare the eschatology of various civilizations and religions, we shall be able to distinguish three degrees of development. Schematically presented, they look as follows: At the first, most primitive level, there exists no justice; there exists no precise and definitive relationship between the lot of man in the other world and the merits attained in this life.

On the second level [of development] transgressions are punished and good deeds are recompensed, but the sanctions, particularly the punishments, are very severe and disproportionate: the gods are revengeful and ferocious. Responsibility is not clearly a personal one. The punishment to be endured does not serve any other purpose than assuaging the anger of the gods; the guilty one does not profit from it in any way.

At the third level, the gods become good and compassionate; the belief is changed to the point of proposing moderate sanctions which are to serve the purpose of the ultimate correction of the sinner. The sinner is no longer rejected with a sense of hopelessness; his sufferings have a goal: that of accepting the transgressor and ultimately returning him to the community of good souls. At this level the gods may even disappear and all things get together, each with a greater or smaller number of errors on his chest striving toward an ultimate unity.[3]

This very schematic outline by Allendy cannot be over-estimated, for it presents the very essence of the evolution of modern civilization which gradually, by jumps, relapses, retrogressions, and renewed efforts to push forward, did arrive at the beginning of this century at a certain culmination of that individualistic ideal which sees the greatest value of life not in life in general, but in man, in the individual as the only carrier of living values.

This striving toward an ideal through the recognition of man as an individual, as the greatest ethico-psychological force of human functioning, is the humanism which has come up time and again in the history of mankind; occasionally it would appear to have been forgotten, then it would reappear with renewed reassertion. During the history of Judeo-Christian civilization there were periods of great darkness in the history of humanistic individualism, but humanism appeared to have come to stay when the Renaissance let it be known that you cannot submerge the individual and still attain salvation. Even the history of the last thirty years, which seems to remind us how strong and cruel, false and abstract are the ideals of the absolute state, or of the absolute socialized community; even this history of blood and of apparent denial of the humanistic ideal that man is the thing, that it is the individual who matters; even despite the growth of mass movements and disindividualized philosophy and the practice of averages and common denominators; even in this our present-day twi-

[3] *Ibid.*, pp. 67-68.

light of man's freedom and the individual's creative self-assertion, our civilization is still reaching out for the individualistic humanism which was so well represented by the best Christian minds of the sixteenth century and has not yet been emulated.

It is this trend in our civilization that is fundamentally responsible for the birth of the newer psychology, which looks into the psychological depth of man and is inclined to disregard the worship of averages that never lead to the individual, still less permit us to gain any insight into his depth; there is no depth in a common denominator. It is this fundamental striving toward the humanistic ideal that is responsible for the great contrast between modern psychology and traditional penal law, for the latter claims to represent society as a powerful abstraction, as a sovereign whole which is always greater and more valuable than the part. In such a philosophy "the part" is the individual, the person, that very thing which seeks to establish itself as the greatest value in our human world.

The result of this contrast is an endless series of endless misunderstandings between traditional penal law, which must in practice consider the individual less important than the community of which he is a member, and the modern, ever-growing, humanistic ideals which consider the community merely as a unified, more practical servant of the individuals who make it up. The contrast is very strong, the conflict almost fatal. Therefore, we may still find such enormities as the Lord Chief Justice of England testifying before the Royal Commission on Capital Punishment and insisting that a certain vicious murderer who was adjudged insane and committed to Broadmoor for life should have been hanged with deliberate disregard of the statute law and the common law.

Let us take a look into this Broadmoor Institution which for so long was a symbol of the darkest aspects of human wretchedness, and to which the murderer was committed whose death the Lord Chief Justice demanded regardless of law written or unwritten. The history of this institution has recently been published, and it was reviewed with brilliant terseness by the editor of *The American Journal of Psychiatry*, Clarence B. Farrar.[4] Broadmoor is an institution for insane murderers. There are about one thousand murderers there—men and women, mostly wife and child murderers. It has been in existence ninety years. There has been no escape of any dangerous murderer from Broadmoor during the past seventy years, and there was only one successful escape in the whole history of the institution. Hardly any mechanical restraint was ever used in Broadmoor, and when Dr. Hopwood was decorated in 1951 for having transformed Broadmoor into an excellent hospital, "the patients signified their approval of this award at a gathering of inmates and staff by lifting the superintendent, seated in his chair, and carrying him shoulder-high around the hall, singing 'For He's a Jolly Good Fellow.' The doctor admitted later to some nervousness during this demonstration: 'I wasn't too easy—one of those carrying me was an epileptic.' "[5]

It must be noted that these patients-criminals were all adjudged "legally insane," were all presumably "medically insane" also. For if a court of law is satisfied that the given

[4] C. B. Farrar in *The American Journal of Psychiatry* for Nov. 1953, reviewing Ralph Partridge's *Broadmoor: A History of Criminal Lunacy and Its Problems*, London, 1953, pp. 399-400.
[5] *Ibid.*

accused is mentally ill "within the meaning of the law," he must be very ill indeed. The uninitiated might be surprised at the *esprit de corps* displayed by this "insane community" and their ability to be grateful to a chief who is at once their warden and medical guide. Would it not be even more surprising to learn of the following:

It is worth while to mention the high morale of the patients when World War II threatened every part of the British Isles. In September 1939 no preparation had been made for the defense of Broadmoor, and to worsen matters, staff losses began at once as men were called to service. Patient response was immediate. Outside the walls where they had never been allowed before they dug manfully in a sand pit, going and coming through the main gate with no attendant in sight, even Back Block patients vigorously taking part in filling sandbags and stacking them against ground floor windows of their blocks. A patients' voluntary fire brigade, with alarm stations outside as well as inside the walls, served loyally throughout the war despite the obvious opportunities for escape.

In addition to this striking capacity to live a life of unity and community of interest, there seems also to be enough spiritual vitality for creative work and community of effort:

As this book abundantly shows Broadmoor is not an altogether unpleasant place in which to live. Privileges have been enlarged considerably in recent years, and comforts too, including many of the luxurious devices that seem so indispensable nowadays. The patients have their own theatrical organization—they call themselves "The Broadhumoorists." Their shows attract an audience from the public, near and far.[6]

It is also interesting to what extent the sense of belonging may develop even in a peculiar individual with propensities to dramatic truancy.

6 *Ibid.*

In January 1888 a wife murderer escaped and was not retaken. In 1896 he gave himself up in New Orleans, shipped back to England for reincarceration but disappeared at the Liverpool dock. In 1927, an old man knocked at the main gate of Broadmoor. It was the old runaway. His prayer for readmission on the ground that life inside was more comfortable than he had found it outside was granted and he spent the remainder of his days contentedly behind the walls.[7]

All this gives the impression of being almost anecdotal, exceptional, a little strange and not entirely probable. For this is not what the average man, be he the man in the street or the Lord Chief Justice, would believe wife and child murderers would do if treated kindly and not punitively, and if left almost entirely free to live out their human propensities under the protection, guidance, and supervision of understanding medical officers.

Broadmoor stands out today as a testimony of strange things that might come about more often and in many more places if we only dared to face the true psychological secret of criminal behavior, instead of endeavoring to refine the rationalizations of purely punitive measures of the law, with their traditional disregard of the totality of the doer of the dreadful deed.

All this points up the essence of the conflict which is inevitable between psychopathology and the law, between the psychiatrists and those concerned with penal justice. For the average man at times gains the impression that the psychiatrist seeks to let loose the criminal, leaving the honest, peace-loving citizen to paddle his own canoe in a marasmic criminal world.

The average citizen, as well as the prosecutor and the

[7] *Ibid.*

judge, reads into modern psychopathology all this socio-logically naïve and morally untenable and impractical non-sense, only because we all feel unconsciously guilty for any transgression which we are called upon to judge; we feel guilty because in our human state we are fallible and are tempted even as all transgressors are. This is a truth which was not proclaimed first by Freud. Almost seven hundred years before Freud, Thomas Aquinas insisted: ". . . *in qualibet autem voluntate creaturae potest esse peccatum secundum conditionem suae naturae.*" [8] We all are fallible and are prone to do misdeeds for which we not only are re-sponsible but, what is much more important, *feel* respon-sible. This feeling of inner responsibility is something that is very difficult to get at as a rule, for often it is covered by many layers of rebellion, challenge, protest—which all look like self-justified, confirmed criminality.

What happened in the past half-century or so is that the clinical psychopathologist, which means the medical psy-chologist, which means the doctor-psychiatrist, not only brought new psychological insight into what is called the criminal mind, but wittingly or unwittingly offered our humanistic aspirations new tools to work with. These tools are not only new, but they all seem to serve a new pur-pose, and the officer of the law does not mind using these tools provided his traditional purpose is not interfered with. In other words, the penologist might want to say: "We like the way you find out things about all those creatures, and we like to make use of your new ways—but please do not interfere with what we are doing; for what we are doing has stood the test of ages, and we do not want to see it recast for some other and to us very unsatisfactory goal."

[8] *Summa Theologica*, I, qu. 63.

The law qua law is right. It does not want to give up the principle of punishment, even though it is occasionally willing to modify the manner of punishment. What the law fails to see is the curative power of healthy self-punishment which never becomes hostility. And what the law further fails to see is that punishment alone inflicted from outside produces only a hostile response, an intensification of hatred, and consequently the diminution of those healthy, auto-punitive, restorative trends in man, which alone make man capable of inwardly accepting punishment and making salutary use of it.

All this may appear vague and general and abstract to the practicing jurist; all of this is usually presented in the courtroom by psychiatric experts who themselves are but pawns in a conventional system of superannuated rules laid down for psychiatric expert testimony. The result is at times laughable, at times sad, almost always regrettable, because the psychiatric expert is treated either as a hireling who must follow the whim of the prosecutor, or as an intruder who works to interfere with the regular course of justice. Hirelings are always used but seldom respected, and intruders are never welcome. Therefore the psychological atmosphere surrounding the psychiatrist in court is an unpleasant one, and it does not propitiate the work of honest science or real justice. It is this problem that the medical psychologist who is interested in criminology must solve first, before he ever may even start to hope that the true insights of modern psychology can be properly tested by modern criminology.

We all know how intense is the hostility which at times is displayed in our courts between the jurist and the psychiatric expert. A highly respected and very just federal judge once addressed me as I was sworn in as an expert witness: "I don't like doctors; they talk a language which we don't understand. Please, Doctor, bear this in mind and talk plainly so that we can understand you." Everybody smiled contentedly including the jury, except the expert who smiled sheepishly even before he had the opportunity of uttering a word.

A French psychiatrist reported some twenty years ago that one of the parties at a trial was so disgusted with an expert that he shot him.[9] But the death of an expert does not reform expert testimony, any more than the death of a murderer reforms criminals.

It is not a question really of psychiatry *versus* the law. It is more a problem of how to make sure that the expert psychiatric witness will be enabled to do his job without being exposed to the temptation of engaging in a duel with the jurist, of how to protect the expert from the temptation of out-prosecuting the prosecutor or out-defending the defense counsel, and thus to permit him to do his doctor's job with the sober competence and intellectual honesty which must be his. There is no easy solution of this problem in sight. I shall attempt to outline briefly a few suggestions which may prove helpful in clarifying the problem itself and which may serve, perhaps, the purpose of breaking down the thick wall of true misunderstanding that actually exists between psychiatry and the law. It is a misunderstanding of intentions, and a lack of understanding of the principle that the psychiatrist qua physician does not come to the witness stand to judge the law, nor would he come if he were not convinced that he would serve the dictates of his professional conscience by testifying in a given case.

9 Allendy, *op. cit.*, p. 48.

In other words, the psychiatric expert himself may have inner conflicts with regard to the very problems about which he is called to give expert testimony; these conflicts will serve to confuse the issues even more. As you see, the job of the psychiatric expert witness is fraught with inner and outer dangers—these must be removed or he will be expert in name only.

Much has been written on the subject of psychiatric testimony, and I do not intend to review or reiterate what has already been said. My major task I consider the psychology of the issues involved, and it is to this problem that I shall turn now.

7.

SOME SUGGESTIONS ABOUT
PSYCHIATRY AND PSYCHIATRISTS

IN ORDER to understand the role and the spiritual goal of psychiatry in criminology, we must recall and recapitulate a few things which perhaps have been said before, and a few human reactions which people are apt to have and to display whenever psychiatry makes its appearance, so to speak.

We shall mention, but only to disregard, those within and without the profession who claim everything for psychiatry and look upon it as a cure-all, as the great remedy which will ultimately rid us of criminals, of Communism, of injustices social and personal. Such a world made safe for psychiatry would be a rather unsafe world, for there are so many things in this world about which psychiatry knows so much and is able to do so very little.

We know that the traditional moralist is suspicious of psychiatry lest it encroach upon ethical teachings and make them all "a matter of psychology." The jurist, too, does not trust psychiatry, as if it wants to abolish the legal norms in favor of purely psychological ones. It is quite interesting to see how through the ages and through the endless variations of cultural traditions there was always a great deal of anxiety on the part of the priest, as well as the judge, lest the doctor who does not conform to the prejudices of the times subvert human beings and thus make them lose their religious faith, their moral principles, and their civic virtues.

It is singular and not a little puzzling that the healer in our midst is so often suspected of being the enemy of our established virtues, personal and civic.

This is a very important psychological phenomenon, this suspicion with which the doctor is met as soon as he turns his attention to issues other than the temperature of the patient, the color of his urine, or the dryness of his skin. We are almost hopelessly ambivalent about doctors in general (and psychiatrists in particular). We admire our doctors and expect them to be dedicated people, almost omniscient in their vision and inexhaustible in their charity, yet we have always wanted our doctors to be sheltered or removed from the very life we wish them to know so well. There was a time when even an interest in music or poetry on the part of the doctor was considered professionally immoral (Rhazes, in the tenth century).

I do not know why this should be so, but it is. Perhaps we read into our doctors all the ideal virtues we ourselves lack, and at the same time mistrust our own idealizations and are afraid that the tolerance, understanding, and endless charity with which we endow them will permit our own weaknesses to come to expression. Thus, under the sheltering good will of the all-forgiving doctor, we might succumb to our ever-present temptation to be bad, to be unkind, cruel, immoral, illicit—to be everything that is always present within us and held down by our own conscience, the strength of which we at times distrust, or by our own misguided wills, the directions of which we fear. In other words, the idealized doctor is the idealized, dedicated free man who is good of his own choosing, who is charitable because of his endless compassion for human suffering, who is what he is to us only because he wants to be

so—caring not about honors or riches and other worldly en-
dowments. Well, how can we help but distrust our own fan-
tasied doctor? Of course, we do not "believe" in him. When
we are most tempted by our weaknesses, we are most suspicious of the ideally free man-healer.

This, I think, is the major reason why doctors were considered out of bounds when they became interested in witchcraft and tried to prove that there were no witches, but
only some people who were accused of being witches and
others who were mentally sick and believed themselves to
be witches. Whenever doctors became psychiatrists and
claimed as part of their sphere of professional work such
fields as education and criminology, they were met with
suspicion, open distrust, and considerable hostility. Priests,
lawyers, judges—all voiced violent disapproval during the
early days of psychiatric beginnings, during the sixteenth
century; and even today this hostility, less overt at times,
is still very definite, very potent, and very patent.

Our courtrooms still lend themselves well to the expression of this hostility toward psychiatry. The psychiatrist is
treated with considerable scorn. His knowledge is chal-
lenged on the questionable ground that psychiatrists disagree so often on points presented to them. Psychiatry
should presumably be discarded just because there are so
many differences of opinion among psychiatrists. If difference of opinion should become a legitimate cause for dis-
paraging the knowledge of those who express these opinions,
there might be no physics, since there is considerable dis-
agreement among Newton, Einstein, Heisenberg, and De
Broglie. We should discard all lawyers, because lawyers
always disagree. We should discard all religious traditions,
because so many theologians disagree on so many things.

We should discard as worthless all great pieces of literature, because so many people disagree on their value. We should throw out most of the musical heritage of the world, because at one time or another Wagner was hated as much as liked, Beethoven, Tschaikovsky, Brahms were considered wild by some and glorious by others. We should forget Aristotle because a Thomist would certainly disagree with a positivist on the importance of Aristotle, although both seem to use him. No, differences of opinion are neither a measure nor even a sign of weakness of a given scientific or philosophic or artistic or religious discipline.

Moreover, what happens to psychiatrists in the courtroom is actually not a clash of opinion but a clash of lawyers, with psychiatrists in the role of baseball bats. The question is not why psychiatrists disagree, but why they are forced to be baseball bats, and why they accept the role of baseball bats.

This is a very serious question. Many factors are responsible for this sorry state of affairs. First, the usual questions propounded in court cannot be considered psychiatric questions. The psychiatrist is asked whether a given person knew the difference between right and wrong; this is not a psychiatric question. The psychiatrist is asked about the legal insanity and responsibility of a given person; these are not psychiatric questions. These become particularly dangerous questions when the psychiatrist is expected to accept the legal definition of insanity because it is legal, and then use his scientific knowledge which more often than not is fully opposed to the legal definition.

It is at this moment that the psychiatrist is forced into the position of choosing between two standards; squeezed as it were by two forces—legal and scientific—he soon finds that he cannot straddle and that he must choose one or the other standard. Not infrequently he is seduced by his quasi-civic propensities and as a wholehearted ally of the law, whatever it is, he puts whatever scientific knowledge and skill he possesses into the service of the legal standard. He then is apt to become a professional witness for the prosecution; he always finds the defendant sane. I know of one such psychiatrist who, after years of such service, happened to testify in a case stating that the defendant was insane. Just before he went to the witness stand, he said to a friend with ill-disguised melancholy, "For the first time in thirty years I will be on the wrong side." The psychiatrist in question was honestly sad, for to testify for the defense meant to him to be on the wrong side.

A great many psychiatric experts find themselves in the same psychological situation. They are most comfortable when they are on the side of the prosecutor of a given misdeed. These psychiatrists are not dishonest doctors; they, like prosecuting attorneys, consider themselves capable of doing just this job of prosecution. The greatest majority of them, I dare say, are not real clinicians who treat sick people most of the time. In this respect, the many and various medical practice acts in various states are as much at fault as some of the volunteer psychiatrists who perennially stray away to the prosecutor's desk. For the law as a rule does not demand that the psychiatric expert be a clinical psychiatrist, or any kind of psychiatrist. Even in those states like New York, which grant certain physicians the certificate of QP (Qualified Psychiatrist), the standards are more or less arbitrary. The old tradition that any M.D. after a certain number of years could become a psychiatric expert witness stands legally unchallenged and professionally unconquered.

It is not surprising, therefore, that there is a great deal of confusion in the field; surgeons who do not know any psychiatry at all, pure neurologists and internists are permitted to testify as psychiatric experts. If such an expert does not show any special qualifications, the prosecutor will call attention to his great experience; if the opposing expert happens to be recognized by his specialty and is a member of many scientific organizations, the prosecutor is apt to call him "a mere joiner," as if a scientific society were an athletic club.

Should a given expert find himself more under the influence of his clinical knowledge than under the pressure of the arbitrary, legal psychiatric concepts, he is apt to be looked upon as a rebel who fights the law and wants criminals "to go scot-free," rather than as a doctor who wants to serve justice.

As I write I feel both humble and a little discouraged for I find it difficult to rid myself of the awareness that the words I use are almost trite, monotonously the same words that have been used for so many generations. The very monotony of it all should suggest that we are dealing here with a very stable, hard-to-move set of institutions and prejudices, and that psychiatry must admit that it is rather helpless in the face of this stability. An unkind disposition might be tempted to call it stagnancy; a patient disposition would be inclined to consider it the dead weight of ritualized tradition—in this case the tradition of legal revenge.

The role of the psychiatrist in the courtroom is still sorely misunderstood because the law moves so very slowly, and it distrusts the "impetuosity" of psychiatrists who would change the laws as often as almost every two hundred years. We in our civilization seem to be satisfied with the thought that we are much further advanced than the Code of Hammurabi, which required the death of a son for the murder of a son, of a daughter for the murder of a daughter. Yet in our gradation of punishments so that each fits the crime, we are not very far from Medieval England where in the County of Lewes the shedding of blood called for a fine of seven pounds, four shillings, while in Shropshire the same transgression called for a fine of forty shillings.[1]

How can we measure crime? Ours is a psychological age, and yet the psychiatrist is confronted with the old, established scales of legal values, and all the psychiatrist is asked to do is to offer precise definitions and accurate tests in support or refutation of the claims of the criminal law. It is a matter of genuine knowledge that such tests do not exist, and I doubt whether they ever will. Accuracy of definition in law is as impossible as it is in psychological measurements of common denominators. There were times when a good and just test was considered the taking of poison: It was once believed by the natives of Madagascar that the innocent would vomit out the poison, while the guilty would succumb, of course. This is reminiscent of the drowning tests for witches: If a suspected woman kept her head above water, she was a witch and could be burned; if she drowned, she was not a witch. It is also reminiscent of some of the refinements of today when drugs are used.

I hope no one will be misled by the apparent harshness of my critical attitude. It is not that the judge, the lawyers, the psychiatrists erring and nonerring are guilty of not doing the right thing. Rather, we are dealing here with a stubborn psychology of human reactions against the evildoers of one's own tribe. The stubbornness of this psychol-

1 Allendy, *op. cit.,* p. 31.

ogy is deeply rooted in the primitive layers of our poorly
domesticated, primitive instincts, and it is difficult for us
to be different.

Let us take a brief look at the historical perspective without which we will not know even how repetitious we are.

Isaac Ray's momentous book on *Medical Jurisprudence
of Insanity* appeared in 1838. Let us glance into pages
written by another doctor half a century later—in January,
1888. It was W. W. Godding, Superintendent of the Government Hospital for the Insane (later St. Elizabeths Hospital) in Washington, D. C., who felt moved to speak before
the Ninth International Medical Congress held in Washington on the subject, "Insanity as a Defense for Crime." [2]
"Insanity," exclaimed Dr. Godding, "is a disease and not
a *dictum*. . . . It can by no possibility become either a
metaphysical conception or a judicial utterance." [3] "While
the physician reasons about disease, the lawyer talks of the
decisions of the court and the answers of the judges, as if
these constituted insanity. They are not arguing from the
same premises." [4]

Dr. Godding is quite scornful, and when he discusses the
jurist's demands that his definition of insanity have substance, he is moved to add that one cannot, of course, object
to the demands of the Oriental princess who wished her
ice to be served warm. "It will not do for us to say that the
psychiatrist's answer is old and trite and has been overruled
again and again from the bench. Content we may be to be
overruled again, we are not content to remain silent." [5]

These are the words of an inspired appeal that psychiatry

---

[2] *The American Journal of Insanity*, Vol. 44, 1887-8, pp. 393 ff.
[3] *Ibid.*, p. 393.   [5] *Ibid.*, p. 393.
[4] *Ibid.*, p. 394.

be recognized for what it is, and not merely as an added device to be linked to the old premises of the law. And it is indeed discouraging to read Godding saying: "I shall not live to see it, but he who writes the history of the twentieth century will record the abolition, among English speaking nations, of my Lord Coke's venerable dogma of a knowledge of right and wrong as a test of criminal responsibility." [6] And further, discussing punishment: "The world may well dispense with a protection that does not protect, with ghastly examples which do not deter other insane men from crime." [7]

Again I must point out how instructive it is, in a sad way to be sure, to take notice that the above admonitions of Godding and the appeals to reason made by Isaac Ray some fifty years previously sound so much alike, and that my own mode and manner of reasoning and appealing is textually almost the same today, nearly three-quarters of a century after the appeal of Dr. Godding.

We may assume of course a grossly pragmatic position and say that since psychiatry has failed to convince jurisprudence during the past century or so, there must be some fundamental weakness in the argument of psychiatry, and that is the reason for its failure. We might also say that there must be something to the argument in which psychiatry persists since it seems to show no signs of weakening, no signs of giving in, still less of giving up. Argue as we may in any direction we choose, the fact remains that such concessions as the New Hampshire law and the Briggs law in Massachusetts are more or less procedural concessions—im-

[6] *Ibid.*, p. 397.
[7] *Ibid.*, p. 399.

portant ones to be sure, but the inner conflict between law and psychiatry remains unresolved.

You will recall that when we tried to reduce the terms "the nature and quality of the act" to their logical and psychological substance, we were inevitably led to issues of a moral nature; that is to say, the primary source, the mainspring of law is morality, individual and public, and there is no justice without morality. However, whenever a system becomes formalized, procedure itself and technicalities of form and decorum acquire a greater importance than they actually deserve.

It so happens that psychiatry cannot be formalized either as a clinical system, or as a method of treatment. When a formalistic clinical attitude is assumed in psychiatry, the psychiatrist loses his usefulness as a healer; but strange as it may seem, he may gain in stature as a psychiatric expert. For if he feels that he can classify mental diseases with precision, and if he feels he can look upon the individual as the sum total of so many logical categories and formal principles, he can fit himself and his opinions perfectly into the mold of the verbal metaphysics of certain aspects of the law. On the other hand, psychiatry will never be able to abandon its search for the individual in the individual person, and therefore psychiatry will always be confronted with the fact that every individual is unique, that no matter how many general laws of human psychology we may discover we must take our general knowledge and distill out of it that very individuality and uniqueness which make up the person whom we study.

Psychiatry is therefore predestined to reject categories and preconceived notions and legal tests. Therefore, psychiatry by the very nature of its subject matter and its method of study is bound to represent itself only, and not one side or the other in an adversary proceeding. In other words, psychiatry cannot really take sides, no matter how much the contingencies and vagaries of our existence push us into the position of experts for one or the other side.

Therefore, both ideally and by the very nature of its scientific method and interests, psychiatry is fit always to appear as a friend of the court. To be sure, the Constitutional rights of the defendant must be protected, but they are hardly protected by our ingenious system of hiring two or more psychiatric baseball bats and lining them up against each other on different sides of a predetermined legal line of separation. The Constitutional rights of the defendant would be amply protected by the right to cross-examine the psychiatric expert, who as a friend of the court would render a well-substantiated report on his findings in a given case. To stress and underscore the need of having a psychiatrist on each side of the battle line is equivalent to assuming in advance that you can always hire an expert to do your bidding; and you always can—for the life we lead is the life we make.

This principle of an expert for each side is a corrupting, immoral principle, and it is difficult to imagine how one concerned with justice could even assume that justice, which is the highest form of morality, could be achieved by means of immoral principles. I hold no brief for the venality of those in the medical profession who are unable to see the immorality of the present system of psychiatric expert testimony, but we must never forget that you will always find a customer for any kind of merchandise, and of course you can always buy anything once you set your mind on obtaining it.

Perhaps this is as good a place as any to consider once more the fundamental issue between psychiatry and the law as it is constituted today. Let us take a closer look at this issue before we try to see what can be done to remedy the sorry situation.

As Dr. Godding put it, the lawyer and the doctor start from different premises. The psychiatrist does not necessarily have to conclude that every criminal is a mentally ill person; the psychiatrist by the very nature of his interest and occupation tries to find out how the mind of the criminal works, how he is led to commit an act of transgression and how, if possible, such acts could be prevented. The psychiatrist, if he were given a chance to study the defendant thoroughly, might acquire knowledge which could be of inestimable value to the judge and to society.

One of the most valuable things which modern psychiatry has discovered is the presence of a conscience in every criminal, no matter how brutal the crime; the presence of a sense of guilt in every criminal, no matter how carefree and callous he might appear; and the presence of a sense of community of interests, of group cohesiveness, no matter how antisocial he might appear. Then, too, modern psychiatry has discovered that the deeper motivations for criminal behavior are aggression which is not fully integrated and socialized, and the considerable degree of egocentricity, of narcissism, which makes any delinquent a lone wolf even if he is a member of a group, a person not fully able to love others, a person lacking in altruism.

It is in the mass of these findings that the psychiatrist discovers himself touching upon the very secret of human values; he discovers that insight into the deeper psychology of man brings him into close contact both with the intimate sources of human brutality and the loftiest problems and sources of human morality. It is this contact that makes the psychiatrist so vulnerable; it is very difficult indeed to be touching the uncharted and unexplored depths of human baseness and human greatness without giving in at times to the temptation of appearing the very master, the mega-lomanic psychological manager of man and even mankind. Luckily, not many among us succumb to this temptation, for the very intimate contact with the inner nature of man inevitably leads to a certain wonderment and humility akin to the one experienced by such great scientists as Heisen-berg or De Broglie, who as a result of their deep scientific insight into natural phenomena perceived how unpredict-able the spontaneous functioning of nature and man is, even though man might appear strong and prophetic by building atomic and hydrogen weapons.

Neither the present system of expert testimony nor the avowed goals of present criminal law provide for a proper presentation of the psychiatric point of view in the court of law. One may say without a moment's hesitation that despite the appearance of so many psychiatrists on the wit-ness stands in our criminal courts, the psychiatric point of view has not yet been fully presented in open court. Our legal procedure is against it. Our psychiatric ability to dem-onstrate our findings in terms which others demand from us is, to say the least, limited. Only the most radical reform of our court procedure would open the door for a more direct presentation of the major psychological issues in-volved in criminal behavior.

We cannot expect such a reform soon, if at all. Dr. God-ding hoped that the twentieth century would make a radical step forward. Half of that century has already gone by, and here and there some experts are permitted to testify as to the unconscious reactions of the accused—but I am afraid that the hope, if any, will lie in the twenty-first century, Dr. Godding's aspirations and our efforts to the contrary notwithstanding.

The very many issues on which we have touched, and the ones we here discussed in greater detail, could be reduced and simplified without doing injustice to scientific truth as follows:

The psychiatrist of today finds himself in great need of a fuller hearing by the law. He has more to say and to reveal about those who commit crimes than he is allowed to say and reveal. He is eager to convince the court and jury that mentally sick criminals deserve an opportunity to live, if not the opportunity to get well. He wants to convince the court and the jury that our knowledge as to who is mentally ill, and as to who knows without really knowing, and as to who acts seemingly rationally but actually not reasonably, has grown to such an extent during the past fifty or seventy-five years that the law must find ways and means of admitting the psychiatrist's views into open court. The American Bar Association and the American Law Institute have given evidence of trying to understand the demands of psychiatry and meet some of its wishes. Those demands, be it underscored again and again, are of a moral nature. They come from the humanism of psychiatric knowledge. The psychological and spiritual picture of these demands is akin to if not identical with similar demands which have been made since Johannes Weyer started the medico-psychological battle against the persecution of witches some four hundred years ago.

Here and there it is believed that if the court were permitted to appoint the psychiatric expert, we would be rid, at least in part, of the shameful and sham battle of experts. The State of Wisconsin has had a statute since 1921 giving the courts the right to appoint the expert. The Uniform Expert Testimony Act, which is incorporated in the Model Code of Evidence of the American Law Institute, has been before the legal and medical professions for over fifteen years; it has thus far been adopted only by the State of Vermont.[8] Winfred Overholser, reviewing this particular situation in the first series of Isaac Ray Lectures, which were given at Harvard University in 1952, was moved to recall Maudsley's remark: ". . . Our legal dignitaries have not the least desire to be helped out of their dilemma." [9]

Overholser also reminds us of a recent pronouncement of the Illinois Supreme Court, to the effect that "while physicians are better qualified to testify to a diseased condition than a layman, their testimony upon the subject of the mental capacity of an individual whom they have been privileged to observe is not entitled to any greater weight than that of laymen." [10] There you are. Of course, not all the courts and not all jurists subscribe to this opinion of the Illinois Supreme Court, but we see clearly that even if all the courts were to take over the job of appointing psychiatric experts, things would not improve very much. The psychological atmosphere remaining what it is, mere procedural ventilation will not clear it.

The whole process of advancing the course of humanistic medical psychology seems to be so very slow under the best

[8] Winfred Overholser, *The Psychiatrist and the Law*, Harcourt, Brace, 1953, p. 125.
[9] Maudsley, quoted by Overholser, *loc. cit.*
[10] *Ibid.*, p. 127.

circumstances. Therefore, it would tax one's optimism a great deal indeed to believe that the law would yield to any pressure other than that of truly inspired scientific knowledge, brought forth by men who would have the courage to make the sacrifices required regardless of the rigidity of established tradition. Here and there one finds an exceptional judge who is not afraid to be enlightened by medical psychology, and who is not afraid that medical psychology might affect his loyalty to the law. Yet the predominant moods of our courts stand unreformed and, I am afraid, unresponsive. It seems to me, therefore, that the psychiatric profession alone must shoulder the responsibility for the reform, that the solution of the problem must lie, as it has throughout the history of medical psychology, in the hands of the psychiatrist himself.

Let us imagine then that the psychiatric profession as represented, for instance, by the American Psychiatric Association, cognizant of the moral soil in which it is deeply rooted, decides to formulate its own moral code which would govern every psychiatrist in good standing and at the same time establish definite scientific medical standards which one must attain to be qualified as a psychiatric expert. It would then become known, to the legal profession and to the public, which psychiatrists the psychiatrists themselves considered qualified as specialists in the field of forensic psychiatry. Psychiatrists might then adopt the following rules of professional conduct.

No qualified psychiatric expert may appear for any one side in a criminal trial; he may not respond to the call of either the prosecution or the defense; he may appear only as a friend of the court. The psychiatrist—qualified to be a forensic psychiatrist—would act against the ethical principles of the profession if he accepted the concept of legal insanity; for clinical psychiatry does not know of such a condition, never saw it, and after almost two hundred years of clinical investigations seriously doubts its existence. The psychiatric expert would be further considered as acting against the ethical code of his profession if he undertook to give an opinion as to the responsibility or irresponsibility of the accused. These are either purely moral or purely legal questions. The psychiatrist on the witness stand may not use his medical prestige and authority to help the moralist who is willing to pass judgment, or to help the courts or the jury to lean in a direction about which a clinical psychiatrist knows nothing except insofar as he is a man and a citizen. On the witness stand, he is only the man of clinical knowledge, a knowledge which he is willing to share with the court and the jury within the hearing of the prosecutor and defense counsel.

Should these principles of ethics be adopted, it would not be difficult, nor immoral, nor illegal to refuse to answer any hypothetical question, which is usually propounded today after the jurist and the expert have worked it all out and composed it in advance. The hypothetical question, let us admit it, is a logical monstrosity, an artificial and pompous creation of the human mind, which wishes to get as far away as possible from reality and from the living human being and talk about both as if they do not exist in fact and decide what to do with both in fact. I have always considered the hypothetical question immoral in all its aspects and I have but one answer for it: I do not know what to say about anything that we may assume has happened, or anybody whom I am asked to assume to be. As a psychiatrist I was taught to look at people and things with the eyes and mind of a trained clinical physician. As a doctor, I know nothing about make-believe, and I was taught by the whole history of my specialty to observe facts and people and not supposition made-to-order, and badly made to boot.

The code of ethics for psychiatric experts thus visualized would in no way put any mentally ill criminal in jeopardy, for all the volunteer, self-appointed psychiatric experts, and the self-qualified medical selectees of some prosecutors and some defense counsels, would automatically disappear from the courtroom, except as onlookers. Juries would be unwilling to lend credence to a man who, whether an M.D. or not, did not comply with the code of ethics of his own profession or who did not even belong to the psychiatric profession, who failed to qualify properly to take the witness stand as a psychiatric expert. Automatically, the pre-established "double standard" of psychiatric opinion would disappear. Automatically, too, would disappear that psychological jeopardy as a result of which not the scientific knowledge and prestige of the given psychiatric expert is awakened, but his human egocentricity, his unwillingness to be made a butt of the ill-humor or unjust sarcasm of the contending sides. Automatically, therefore, the psychiatric expert would be relieved from the pressure of cheap human passions and the defensive and self-defensive maneuvers to which anyone who is attacked in public is bound to resort. It is common knowledge that even under the wisest guidance of a most impartial judge the humiliation to which experts are subjected, and the psychological counterattacks by the experts, are almost always a part of a criminal trial, particularly if this trial happens to attract public attention and arouse public opinion.

The Constitutional rights of the accused, as I have

pointed out, would not be put in jeopardy by such a projected code of ethics, for neither the prosecution nor the defense would be prevented from examining and cross-examining the psychiatric expert after he had submitted to the court his report based on a personal, clinical study of the accused. I do not visualize this new type of expert as being an appointee of the court as is the custom in France, for instance. I visualize him as a member of a panel of psychiatric experts, made up much in the same manner as a jury panel is made up. The court might offer to the defense and prosecution the list of psychiatric experts. The defense and the prosecution would have the right to make peremptory challenges, as they do when a jury is being selected. Each side might have the right to make, say, two challenges until three psychiatric experts were chosen, sworn in and set to work. Their findings could then be made available to both sides through the judge. Thus, both the defense and the prosecution would be given the same impartial and purely medical information. The three experts would consult with each other, but they need not agree. They might offer a unanimous opinion; they might offer a minority and majority report; they might offer three individual reports.

There would then be plenty of room left to test, verify, examine, and cross-examine the experts. There would not be any animosity created by the sense of split loyalties and personal prejudices.

The added advantage of this new situation would be the fact that the prosecution and the defense would have simultaneously at their disposal the same medico-psychological information, and the silly and pernicious game of one side hiding from the other some particular bit of information would be eliminated, at least as far as the medico-psychological findings are concerned. Scientific, clinical, medical information should automatically be made available to all sides and in open court; it is not the kind of information which justice should tolerate being juggled by lawyers, prosecutors, or defense counsels who in the passion of contention find themselves more fired with the desire to win than to serve the cause of moral or legal justice.

I wish to repeat that, considering the present state of criminal law, the cause of justice both moral and legal weighs heavily on the shoulders of the psychiatric profession, and therefore it is the psychiatric profession which may prove to hold the key that would open the doors of justice more widely.

The issues that I have stressed in these pages more often than any others are the issues arising from the trial and conviction of mentally ill transgressors of the law. But neither I personally nor the psychiatric profession as a whole sees its field of endeavor limited to the issues mentioned, no matter how important these issues are. For we must remember the much greater issue—that of restorative punishment, that of the re-education of the criminal, that of returning the criminal to the community as a full-fledged and rightful member of it, and not merely letting him out of prison and waiting till he is sent back again.

We must bear in mind two things: (1) Of course, a great many criminals may and will prove unredeemable. Many of them will have to stay in a protected environment, protected from themselves and for the protection of the community for the rest of their lives. (2) Criminals cannot be classified on the basis of the type of crime they commit. Because sex offenses are particularly abhorrent to us, we are inclined to consider sex-offenders a particularly bad and dangerous type. This just is not so. There is a sexual element, and a potent one, in almost every criminal act.

Criminals should be classified on the basis of their psychological propensities and the inner structure of their personalities. Neither the law nor the warden is fit to pass on the corrigibility or incorrigibility of a given criminal. Those who mete out the revenge of society on the transgressor are by their nature and training unfit to develop a deep psychological insight into the psychological dynamics of a given criminal's behavior. Only specially trained clinical workers who understand the psychopathology of the nonpsychotic individual can be entrusted with the evaluation of the criminal. I have in mind the criminal who has already passed through the hands of the law and has been transferred to one of the various prisons, some of which are still called penitentiaries and correctional institutions.

You will recall the story of Broadmoor. You will remember how mentally ill patients, people severely compromised psychologically, who are destined to stay the remainder of their lives in that prison-hospital "for criminal lunatics," how those seemingly hopeless wretches were able to display a sense of unity, a sense of social responsibility, a sense of altruistic dedication, even a sense of sacrifice. As I have mentioned, present-day, dynamic medical psychology sees the psychology of the criminal, sees his ill will, in a somewhat different light from the one of some fifty years ago. It sees in the criminal, first, a person whose human, ethico-social potentialities have been stunted or dislocated but usually not destroyed. It also sees in the criminal a person who quite unwittingly responds with aggression to the aggression of the penal law, and therefore finds himself potentially more criminal instead of less as a result of a severe

sentence or very severe treatment in prison. The emphasis,
therefore, as I see it, should be placed on quieting down as
much as possible the autonomous, impulsive, aggressive
drives of the given criminal, and on the propitiation of
those altruistic drives which are stunted within him, or
derailed, as it were, from the path of his social consciousness and behavior.

This brings up the whole problem of penology, the psychology of recidivism, the curative and educative value of
manipulating the punishment not to fit our sense of revenge, but to fit the personality structure of the given
criminal and the specific psychology of his crime. The whole
mass of the complex and burdensome problems of modern
criminology is destined to be revised in the light of modern psychology.

René Allendy, whom I have mentioned before, saw the
greatest curative power in what he called "inner justice,"
and which he saw in the mechanisms of self-punishment
which are operative in man. I do not think I can follow
Allendy the whole distance of his remarkable and eloquent
argument, but I think his view is worth reporting. According to Allendy's observations (and he is right about many
conditions and instances), nothing is more effective than not
treating a transgressor too severely. If we do not threaten
him with revenge, "he stops consciously being afraid of
vengeance on the part of his adversary and, in the obscurity
of his unconscious, he begins to fear the social vengeance
which is alive within him, undefined, diffuse, taking possession of him." [11] Allendy sees the salvation of the transgressor in the ever-present social instincts of man which
lead him to a sense of guilt, to self-punishment. The out-

[11] Allendy, *op. cit.,* p. 258.

sider may never see the inner anxiety of the evildoer, but it could be left to the professional medical psychologist to bring it out, to make it visible, to utilize it as a force for re-education. It is too simple, says Allendy, to believe that the evildoer is happy because he succeeds in doing evil, his appearance to the contrary notwithstanding. The mechanism of self-punishment, Allendy believes, if given time will always take its toll in far greater measure than our legal sanctions and punishments.

Allendy cites an interesting example, even though the events he mentions are no longer subject to precise psychological evaluation. It is to give point to Allendy's main thought that I quote him here:

Under the circumstances it would be a vain undertaking to try and cite many cases; each individual case might not prove anything. May I cite an example of what I would be inclined to believe is a remarkable demonstration of the action of the auto-punitive mechanisms. I have in mind the story of the curious circumstances which seemed to serve as vindication of the Order of Templars for the treatment of some of their predecessors.

The King of France, Philip the Fair, and Pope Clement V got together in order to suppress the too powerful international organization of the Order of Templars, and in order to confiscate their property. An odious accusation against the Templars was raised, an accusation which ultimately brought them to the worst tortures. Stupid confessions were exacted, and about sixty members of the Order were led to the bonfire.

The trial was led by the energetic Guillaume de Nogaret, and it represents one of the most vile and cruel machinations which anyone ever dared to undertake for political and financial reasons. When the Grand Master of the Order was being burned at the Ile de la Cité (in Paris) on March 14th, 1314, he swore that he was innocent, and he prayed that his criminal enemies would be called to answer before the Tribunal of the Lord. One month later, Clement V and Guillaume de Nogaret were dead. Six months later Philip the Fair was also dead. These coincidences did not fail to make a profound impression.[12]

Allendy sees the finger of immanent justice in our social instincts and the self-punitive drives which spring from them. He sees a profound significance in the workings of these drives, which "make a sort of very painful purgatory of our lives on this earth." [13]

The interpretation of the above events may not be correct, but taken as a parable the story is psychologically valid, and one wonders to what extent the law can intelligently manage and administer the problems of crime unless it does take cognizance of the self-punitive drives which play such an enormous role in human behavior.

Here we must admit we have reached a point at which the deeper principles of human morality, of loving one's neighbor, of nonresistance to evil, converge with the deeper psychology of the maturity of the human ego, of altruism, and of human relationships which are not based solely on the pursuit of egocentric drives or passions, no matter how cultivated these drives, no matter how encased they may be in the traditions which lend respectability to human hatred and revenge.

In this connection I would like to record a story which is authentic.

A young New York policeman, aged twenty-six, saw a Negro having a cup of coffee in a luncheonette near the candy store which he owned. The Negro for some reason appeared suspicious to the policeman, who assumed that the Negro had something to do with the traffic in narcotics. The policeman proceeded to search the man, which he had

12 *Ibid.*, pp. 260 f.
13 *Ibid.*, p. 261.

no right to do without a warrant. In the scuffle it came to pass that the policeman's pistol went off, wounding the man, aged thirty-six, in the thigh. In due course the wounded man recovered from his injury; he was also cleared in court of any suspicion of trafficking in narcotics. He then proceeded to sue the City of New York for $475,000 damages for various injuries sustained. The police officer (a white man) had in the meantime been suspended, and he was now on trial on four counts. As the trial opened, the attorney for Mr. Burns, the Negro complainant, stood up and addressed the court from the spectator's seats, one of which was occupied by the complainant.

"The attorney said his client 'seems to be even more concerned about the policeman than he is about the wound he himself received. He is also concerned about the fact that the police officer is a married man and comparatively new in the department.' The attorney said that Mr. Burns . . . is 'even more concerned about . . . better relations and the broad concepts of the brotherhood of man' and asked the court to grant the defendant 'every conceivable indulgence'" and try him for the least grave of the four counts. The Judge replied: "'It is an inspiring thing, to those of us who daily have to see bitterness of one person against another, to see a man who is big enough . . . to appeal for the man who has wronged him. It is almost Biblical in its concept, and the court cannot fail to be impressed by it.'" [14]

The newspaper story does not go on to tell of what guilty feelings the police officer may have developed—nor am I going to assume anything. However, the response of the court is telling, and is a living testimony to the sense of relief the court feels when it is freed from the necessity of following

[14] New York *Herald Tribune,* November 11, 1953.

the dictates of the revengeful bitterness of man or his laws.

By way of further illustration there comes to mind one of the very moving stories of Carl Ewald (1856-1908), the Danish writer who wrote the great and yet almost forgotten classic, *My Little Boy*.[15] In Chapter VII of this book Ewald relates how his little boy was given a penny to buy biscuits needed in the kitchen. The boy went to the bakery, but instead of carrying out his commission he bought candies for himself. The father saw it all from a window across the street. He continues, "And I, who, Heaven be praised, have myself been a thief in my time, run all over the house and give my orders." [16] The boy comes home; he is silent. The father lets the boy confess his crime rather slowly. The father has not the heart to hurt the boy and finally, seemingly by accident, he gives the boy another penny. This time the boy gets the biscuits and brings them to the cook as previously ordered. "He has committed his first crime" is the thought of the father, and he and the boy's mother sit until late at night talking about it and about the power of money. And the thought flashes through the father's mind: "Yet there were two people yesterday who killed a man to rob him of four dollars and thirty-seven cents."

The short and very moving story by Carl Ewald is as old as humanity, yet always new. We were all thieves at one time or another. Those of us who, like the little boy of Carl Ewald, did not grow up to continue to be thieves are very lucky indeed, lucky that we did not turn out to be among those who killed a man to rob him of four dollars and

15 Carl Ewald, "My Little Boy," Chapt. VII, pp. 289-92 in *The Scribner Treasury*, Charles Scribner's Sons, 1953.
16 *Ibid.*, p. 289.

thirty-seven cents. By "lucky" I do not mean a play of fate, a felicitous concatenation of circumstances, a number of lucky breaks. What I mean by "lucky" is that that little boy was fortunate enough to be truly loved, fortunate enough to love in return, and therefore to sense the pangs of pain which both his father and his mother tried not to display. He was fortunate that his father recalled that he too had once been a thief when a little boy, and that this father did not permit his anxiety to become an overbearing, paternal, self-righteous hatred. That little boy, I repeat, was lucky in that on the day of his first crime he was loved and was able to love in return, and his father was right when he said to himself: "He has committed his first crime. He has understood it."

In our early years we can be shaped by love; what makes us so malleable is not the sentimental attitude of gushing parents, but that loving attitude which does not arouse our ever-present hatred (mostly unconscious) to intense aggression. It is in the soil of aggression that certain ethico-social transformations take place, and some of them branch off in the form of delinquency and crime—human phenomena which we all hate, which we must hate as moral human beings and as members of society. Unfortunately, we turn this our legitimate hatred more often than not on the person rather than the deed, and hence the perennial conflict between psychiatry and law.

I find no better words with which to conclude these pages than those of M. B. Sampson, who said in the preface to his *Rationale of Crime:*

> In sending forth the present edition, the author is desirous of requesting a continuance of the indulgence already received. He does not seek indulgence for his opinions, for if these are errone-

ous, he desires that they may be refuted; and if they are true, as he believes them to be, it is out of the power of any individual to retard their recognition. But, in stating views wholly subversive of many deeply-rooted ideas which have long been maintained by abler minds, it is next to impossible, while an attempt is made to express them with clearness and force, to present them in a style entirely free from all appearance of arrogance or presumption; and what he would ask is, that his readers should estimate this difficulty, and do him the justice to believe that it has been his anxious endeavour to avoid it. In his own mind, he feels certain that the views which he has stated must, sooner or later, overturn the present system for the treatment of criminals.

INDEX

[137]